READYMADE HOME FURNITURE

Easy Building Projects Made from Off-the-Shelf Items

COOL
SPRINGS
PRESS

Inspiring | Educating | Creating | Entertaining

Brimming with creative inspiration, how-to projects, and useful information to enrich your everyday life, Quarto Knows is a favorite destination for those pursuing their interests and passions. Visit our site and dig deeper with our books into your area of interest: Quarto Creates, Quarto Cooks, Quarto Homes, Quarto Lives, Quarto Drives, Quarto Explores, Quarto Gifts, or Quarto Kids.

Library of Congress Control Number: 2018952181

Acquiring Editor: Mark Johanson
Project Manager: Jordan Wiklund
Art Director: Brad Springer
Photography: Rich Fleischman
Layout: Kim Winscher
Photo Assistance: Eric Smith, Ian Miller
Author: Chris Peterson

Printed in China

NOTICE TO READERS

For safety, use caution, care, and good judgment when following the procedures described in this book. The publisher and BLACK+DECKER cannot assume responsibility for any damage to property or injury to persons as a result of misuse of the information provided.

The techniques shown in this book are general techniques for various applications. In some instances, additional techniques not shown in this book may be required. Always follow manufacturers' instructions included with products, since deviating from the directions may void warranties. The projects in this book vary widely as to skill levels required: some may not be appropriate for all do-it-yourselfers, and some may require professional help.

Consult your local building department for information on building permits, codes, and other laws as they apply to your project.

CONTENTS

CONTENTS

Built-Ins from Stock Cabinetry 104

Metric Conversion Chart. 142
Index 143

Introduction

Why the endless fascination with hardware stores and home centers? Why are home craftsmen and craftswomen, and even the least experienced DIYer among us, drawn to the local hardware store as if in a trance? It doesn't seem to matter if it's a mom-and-pop operation crammed between the ice cream shop and pharmacy downtown, or the big box home center that has its own exit off the interstate. The allure is there regardless and even when you don't actually need anything. But what is that allure? Just what is it about hardware stores?

The answer can be summed up into one word: possibilities.

Those possibilities come in two flavors—piece-by-piece and complete packages. A hardware store is actually a little like a well-stocked supermarket: you can buy all the ingredients you need to create something really wonderful that is completely yours, or you can buy an already completed creation. The "already completed" purchases, such as tool chests, lighting fixtures, and screen door kits, are certainly interesting and useful, but they are just one part of this book.

In fact, this book is about all the bits and pieces that can be put together in new and ingenious ways to create home furnishings and accents that are at once useful, fun, unique, and economical. That includes both fully complete structures like prefab cabinetry and materials that can serve as one component in a greater structure, such as vinyl or wood crown molding. This book is about recipes that make the most of all those bits and pieces you might find on a scavenger hunt in a home center and hardware store aisles.

And although the projects in the pages that follow may use home center staples in ways that they were never intended to be used, those projects don't include arcane materials. Everything incorporated here can be found at any well-stocked hardware store. We've been careful not to include special-order items, or those that come in sizes not commonly stocked. The focus here is on fun, not frustration.

The emphasis is also on creativity. As you read through these projects and pick one or two (or more) to tackle in your own workshop, keep in mind that these are explicitly designed to be adaptable. You can change measurements to fit your own home spaces and needs, swap out different materials as appropriate and available, and finish your creations in a way that suits your own sense of style. Never fear to customize any of these. Of course, you can always craft them just as intended. The designs have been developed to suit a wide range of interior styles and looks. Although it's the nature of hardware projects to look more industrial than traditional, all the projects are meant to be subtle enough that you don't have be a fan of steampunk to appreciate the looks.

These projects are also designed with the novice in mind. None require specialized expertise or tools, and they can all be built with just a modicum of attention to detail, patience, and elbow grease—resources every homeowner has at his or her disposal.

Every aisle in a hardware store offers the promise of some new, ingenious creation just waiting to be designed and built.

Beyond the design styles, the lineup of projects has been developed to include something for every room in the house. It doesn't matter if you're looking for a new workspace in the corner of a guest bedroom, a totally organized all-in-one structure for your out-of-control laundry room, or even a sturdy arm chair that can do your living room proud and find a home on the patio as well—you'll find all that in the pages that follow. Oh, and much, much more.

So pick a creation that meets your needs and preferences, and then use it as an excuse for yet another trip to your local, oh-so-appealing hardware store (or a lost Saturday afternoon in that home center down the way). Fun and home improvement satisfaction in equal measure await you in those aisles.

The Hardware Store Primer

Mixing and matching home center or hardware-store materials in interesting and useful projects requires an understanding of the basics in each aisle, all those materials that could go into making any project successful. It also means knowing what tools are best for the job at hand and how best to use them. The projects featured in this book require a balance of creatively combining dissimilar materials with tried-and-true construction methods that will ensure the integrity and longevity of anything you build.

The best materials for these types of projects are durable, resistant to wear and abuse, and easy to modify. Although there are obvious candidates that pop out at you in any tour of a home center—wood shelving, cabinetry, common fasteners, brackets—it's wise to keep your eye and your mind open to more unusual choices that can fill the bill. You'll probably be surprised at where your imagination leads you. For instance, PEX pipe could be used to craft a funky and eye-catching spiral tomato cage for the garden, or as a decorative accent on a larger project. Go down every aisle in the hardware store with fresh eyes and no preconceptions and you'll be surprised how many possibilities become apparent.

No matter what materials might go into what you're building, they have to be put together in a way that makes structural sense. When it comes to creating stable, lasting, and safe projects for the home, proper fastening is key. That's why we start here with the hardware that holds other pieces together.

FASTENERS

There are many, many ways to fasten one part of a project to another, and any decent hardware store will stock most all of them. Picking the best fastener and fastening method is crucial to the security and integrity of whatever you build. The method you choose will be dictated by whether you're joining like materials, or completely different bits and pieces, the inherent stresses in the design, the use for which the project is intended, and other factors.

Nails and screws. Nails are easy to use, hold fairly well, and are available in a vast number of sizes, types, and styles to suit a wide range of applications. However, screws are more precise, provide greater longevity, and are easier to remove without damaging project materials. That's why although finishing nails are still the best choice for many basic wood-to-wood joints where appearance is very important, screws will inevitably be the better option for the type of projects featured in this book. The challenge is selecting exactly the screw that will do the job best; there are an awful lot of types from which to choose.

Screw Types

Slotted

Phillips

Pozidriv®

Square-drive (Robertson)

Hex-drive

Torx

Drywall screws are an all-purpose, popular go-to option for many home craftsmen working on their own creations. Problem is, they strip easily and can be hard to drive into certain materials and situations—not to mention their tendency to snap when driven into dry lumber. It seems like there has to be a better all-purpose fastener.

These days, there is. Even small hardware stores now stock wonderful modern screw alternatives. Known generically under their brand names such as Spax and GRK, these fasteners feature innovative designs that have redefined what multi-application screws can be. Most feature Torx-drive or Pozidrive heads, styles that are far less likely to strip than Phillips or standard slot-head screw designs. These screws are specially designed with threads that alleviate the need for pilot holes and, in some cases, for countersinking. Torx heads have a distinctive star-drive head, while Pozidrive features a sturdier version of the Phillips head; both are incredibly strong gripping.

Regardless of the type of screw you choose, size matters. As a general rule of thumb, any screw should penetrate at least half the thickness of the material serving as the base. Screws are also organized by thickness or *gauge*. Gauges range from #2 to #16; #8 is the most common and the most useful in the type of general construction used in the projects here. However, #12 is a good choice if you're using especially thick or heavy material, and finer work may call for #6. The screws are categorized by length within the gauges.

Nuts and bolts. As long as both sides of the material being fastened are accessible, a nut and bolt can be a super-solid, permanent way of joining even very dissimilar materials. However, bolts are generally more awkward to work with than screws. There are different styles of bolts with different head shapes, but most are clunky and apparent, which can make them a poor choice for applications where looks matter (unless

Machine Bolts

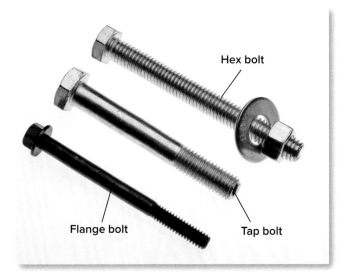

Hex bolt

Flange bolt

Tap bolt

you're going for an industrial vibe). The projects in this book rarely use these types of fasteners.

Glues and adhesives. For such a simple concept—a liquid that dries to bond two material surfaces together—there is an incredible diversity of adhesives available inside even the most modest hardware store. In most structural situations, adhesive or glues are not used alone; the holding strength just isn't as great as a physical connection such as a screw. Most adhesives are also inefficient or completely incapable of bonding dissimilar materials. That said, they have their place in some projects.

Wood glue is a handy option for wood-to-wood bonding. You'll find three grades of wood glue: Type 1 that is applicable for interior and some mild exterior uses (some level of water resistance); Type 2, for exterior applications; and Type 3, which is meant for interior use only. As the name implies, wood glues are not very good at bonding wood with plastics or metal. For that, you'll need a more versatile adhesive.

Cyanoacrylate is a class of multi-purpose glues that works on many different materials

Some of the adhesives useful in home carpentry include carpenter's wood glue, exterior carpenter's glue, liquid hide glue, polyurethane glue, panel adhesive, latex caulk, silicone caulk, and a hot glue gun with glue sticks.

(although the holding strength varies, depending on the material being bonded). The most common of these is known generically as super glue. Cyanoacrylates can be effective over small surface areas, but are not regularly used in projects such as the ones in this book. That's because they are tricky to work with; they set quickly and are difficult to clean up or remove once they dry and cure. They also have a minimal shelf life—about one year unopened.

Epoxies are some of the most useful adhesives. Most are two-part formulas that require speed and precision to use, but provide superior holding strength. Some can be used as gap fillers, and epoxies can be good choices for bonding dissimilar materials.

Polyurethane glues are interesting modern choices for eclectic projects. Initially hyped as the ultimate construction glue, polyurethane products may not totally live up to the hyperbole, but they do offer a lot of advantages. They are usually

used in wood-to-wood mating, are sandable and stainable, and have impressive holding strength. They can also be used to fill gaps.

Construction adhesive is a general-purpose product meant to hold varying materials together, such as sticking vinyl molding to wood board. You'll find sub types like panel adhesive, meant for what the name denotes. These aren't, however, the best choice for pure strength and long-term holding power when it comes to projects like furniture. Any type of construction adhesive is more often used as in tandem with another method of fastening, such as screwing or nailing.

Certain guidelines apply regardless of the adhesive you're using. Unless you're completely familiar with the glue or adhesive, always test it first on scraps of the materials you'll be bonding. Be clear on the proper cleanup method for the adhesive, and read and follow all safety recommendations. Before you use an adhesive, make sure the surface is clean of dirt, grease, or any debris such as sawdust. Any adhesive bond is reliant on full and unimpeded contact with connecting surfaces.

Zip ties. These are handy, if somewhat unattractive, fasteners best used for materials of unusual shapes that need to be secured together (like pipes crossing in an X or a T). Zip ties come in a full range of lengths and, even though they are incredibly strong, it's easy to cut them with a sturdy pair of scissors. They are simple to use, don't degrade, and they will tolerate shifting and various stresses and strains over time. They are not, however, as useful or convenient for bonding one surface directly to another as other options.

JOINING SPECIFIC MATERIALS

Every material is most easily bonded with similar materials. But there are chemical and physical ways to join dissimilar surface materials.

Plastic. Plastic-to-plastic bonds are often made with adhesives because there are so many bonding agents to choose from. The table below lists the best.

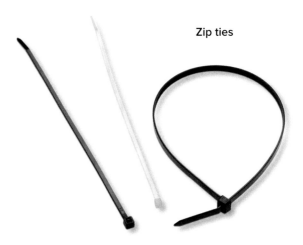

Zip ties

Keep in mind that unlike wood, plastic is not one type of material—there are actually many different plastics. This complicates bonding any given plastic surface. For instance, PVC pipes are fastened to other PVC pipes with cement, but the correct cement must be used; there are different types for PVC, CPVC, ABS, and different schedules of plastic pipes (and, unfortunately, the tins they come in all look the same). That's why it is especially important to put on the reading glasses when shopping for adhesives for plastic, and closely follow the recommendations and instructions on the label.

A SHORT AND QUICK PRIMER TO PLASTIC ADHESIVES

ADHESIVE:	IDEAL USE:	DRAWBACK:
Epoxy	Strong permanent bond; anywhere user control over hardening is desired; holds in wet conditions	Messy and requires precision
Cyanoacrylate	Stationary parts; low torsional resistance	Outdoor use; bond will weaken under repeated extreme temperature swings
Acrylic Adhesive	Exceptional bonding strength similar to epoxy	Fast acting, little room for error
Solvent Cement	Only on plastic-to-plastic mating; permanent, unbreakable bond	Have to match proper solvent to type of plastic; will not work with other materials
Urethane	Wherever flexible bond is desired; great for mating plastic to other materials	Weaker than other adhesives, never hard; can be a challenge to cure correctly

Metal. Walk down any hardware store aisle and you'll come across many different types of metal. Expanded metal sheet. Sheet metal joist hangers. Iron L brackets. Diamond plate. All of these can be handy in reinforcing a project. Joining one to another can be done quickly and permanently by high-temperature welding. But let's face it: welding is dangerous, complicated, technical, and won't work for certain dissimilar metals. Not to mention, most people don't have a welding rig parked in the corner of their garage. That's why none of the projects in this book mention welding.

In the vast majority of cases, the easiest way to attach metal to any material—including another metal surface—is physical fastening. That means screwing or bolting the pieces together. You'll find more on metal-drilling bits on page 17.

Wood. Joining wood to wood is one of the most common steps in home DIY projects. Wood is naturally an accommodating material: cheap and easy to modify. Wood can be laminated to other wood with wood glue, a combination of glue and fasteners, or fasteners alone. Although they can be very handy in situations where the wood will not be subjected to extreme torsional forces or rough handling, wood glues are not among the stronger adhesives and many are not even waterproof.

Wood can be nailed to wood, but increasingly nails are only used for finishing work where appearance is paramount. Where holding strength is key, screws are much preferred. Similarly, wood is most often screwed or bolted to other materials in projects that mix and match components. Construction adhesive can be used in preparation for more thorough fastening, but is rarely used alone to attach wood to metal or plastic (or vice versa).

Rubber. Rubber components can be tricky. Rubber washers and pads can be used in projects to counteract potential vibrations—in which case, the rubber will be screwed or bolted to other materials and surfaces. Where the rubber surface is meant to be both structural and decorative, gluing the rubber down may be preferable. Choose an adhesive based on the material to which you're attaching the rubber. In general, use a silicone-based adhesive when joining rubber to metal; use a contact or spray adhesive when joining rubber to plastic or wood.

Fabric. Some projects involve adding fabric panels to a frame or other structure. Fabric can be a wonderful way to personalize a project or add an unexpected look. You'll find some fabrics that will tolerate exposure to the elements, so you can even use them on outdoor projects. There are several ways to secure any fabric in place. Grommet kits are widely available at home centers and hardware stores, are inexpensive, and often include everything you need—the tools as well as the grommets. The kits are simple to use. They involve punching holes along one edge of a fabric panel or sheet, and then reinforcing the holes with metal grommets. The panel or sheet can then be hung or attached to a frame with paracord, twine, cable, or specialized hangers. There is also a quicker, less formal way to attach fabric to a tubular frame. *Snap clamps* are simple plastic sections that clamp over pipe or thick dowels, and can be used to hold fabric in place.

Specialized materials. Adding stone surfaces or oddly shaped pieces to a project usually requires a creative approach. That's where many of the small bits and pieces to be found in the aisles of a home center come into play. For instance, flat, slotted angle irons can be used as support brackets in tandem with bolts and wing nuts to hold a piece of a project in place. It all comes down to adapting a creative solution to any challenge that presents itself.

SECURING PROJECTS TO A WALL, FLOOR, OR OTHER SURFACE

Some projects are designed to be attached to walls, floors, or both. An example is the Utility Organizer on page 30, which would be unwieldy and take up much more floor space if not wall mounted. Other projects should be anchored to the floor or wall to keep them from moving, or make them appear built in, as is the case with the Media Bar on page 130 and the Hobby Center on page 124.

The most stable wall attachment requires finding a stud. Accurately locating studs is an incredibly useful home improvement skill, especially in this modern age of wall-mounted flat-screen TVs and floating shelves that rely on solid connections for their integrity.

To find a stud, you can do the basic "knock" test, by rapping on the wall and listening for the hollow echo of the cavities in between studs.

THE TOOL AISLE: STUD FINDER SHOPPING GUIDE

A stud finder is a handy addition to any homeowner's toolbox, one that requires virtually no skill to use. Prices range from a few dollars to upward of $65. Extra cost buys more reliability, accuracy, digital versus analog performance, and added features.

- **Detection.** What your stud finder can detect is a product of how much it costs. Buy a bargain stud finder and you'll only be able to detect wooden studs (and sometimes not even those, reliably). Spend more and you not only increase the accuracy of the stud finder, you may also be able to find the center of the stud. The most expensive and full-featured units offer reliable detection of unshielded wiring and pipes—as well as determining if pipes are copper or iron. If you're going to be using the stud finder a lot, the ability to detect underlying plumbing and wiring (and avoid any attendant mishaps) is well worth the additional cost.

- **Level.** The three types of level offered relate to the price point of the tool and are the following (from lowest to highest priced): basic bubble level, electronic level, laser level.

- **Screen.** The most basic stud finders have no readout other than magnetic pointers that indicate you're over a nail and a bubble level. More sophisticated options in the middle of the price range will have a series of LED lights that light up or go out the closer or further you get from the center of the stud. Models at the high end have LED screens that approximate what is beneath the wall surface—including differentiating between studs, wires, and pipes.

- **Calibration.** Mid-level and high-priced stud finders must be calibrated. This is a process through which the stud finder determines wall thickness and it sets the tool up for success. If your stud finder has a calibration feature, follow the manufacturer's instructions exactly to ensure that the stud finder operates as accurately as possible.

- **Extras.** The more you spend, the more comfortable the stud finder will be to use. Special grips allow the finder to be held and slid along the wall more easily. Use your judgment as to whether that matters to you. Some stud finders include a "marking" slot or channel, which makes marking the location of screws or hangers especially accurate and easy. Some higher-end units include audible signals that reinforce the visual readout. Generally speaking, these don't add much to the actual accuracy and usefulness of the tool.

However, that is an imperfect method that leads to mistakes more often than not. You can also look closely at baseboard or crown molding, to detect marks where the finish nails were puttied over. That, too, is a rather unreliable method. That's why the best way to locate studs is to head over to the tool department of your local hardware store and start shopping for a stud finder.

Any stud finder is easy to use (although you should always follow the manufacturer's instructions). Turn the unit on unless it is a basic, non-powered model. Calibrate the stud finder if it has a calibration function, then simply move it slowly side to side on the wall until it registers a stud. Mark the location and move onto the next stud as necessary.

Selecting and Using Anchors

Sometimes, fastening to a stud just isn't possible. In those cases, you'll turn to the super useful hardware store staple: the wall anchor. There are many different kinds, all of which can be grouped into two basic categories: Expansion anchors and hollow cavity anchors. Expansion anchors rely on friction to hold them in place and are—depending on the type of anchor and wall—somewhat less secure, reliably holding less weight. Anchors of all types are rated for the weight they can support; those ratings are generally conservative and you should feel confident in following them.

Plastic expansion. These are the simplest, cheapest, and weakest anchors. They should be used only for lightweight hanging, such as pictures. A hole, slightly smaller than the thickest diameter of the anchor, is drilled into the wall and the plastic anchor is pushed or tapped into the hole. When a screw is driven into the anchor, it expands the plastic sides, helping them grip the wallboard.

Threaded. These look like screws, with oversized threads and long tips. You'll find both metal and plastic threaded anchors, but do yourself a favor and avoid the plastic (actually, nylon) versions, which tend to collapse or deform under pressure and can be difficult to remove. To install a threaded anchor, drill a small pilot hole, and then screw the anchor into the wall surface as you would a screw. Threaded anchors are stronger than expansion types and are easier to remove.

Toggles and winged. Both of these use "legs" that open once the anchor is put through wallboard or any wall surface with a cavity behind it. In the case of toggles, the anchor is pushed through a pre-drilled hole and then the legs are spread as the bolt is removed from the anchor. Winged anchors don't have a resident bolt. Instead, they are pushed through a hole and, when

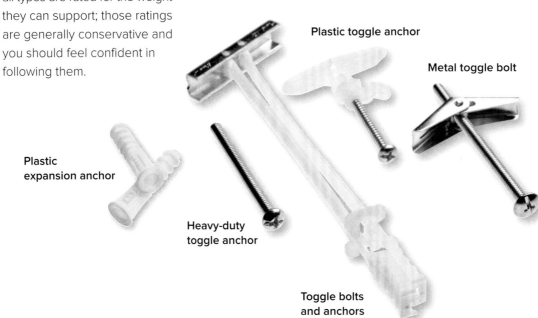

Plastic toggle anchor

Metal toggle bolt

Plastic expansion anchor

Heavy-duty toggle anchor

Toggle bolts and anchors

a screw is driven into the anchor, wings at the base spread to hold the anchor in place. These types of anchors offer a great deal of holding power but are extremely difficult to remove.

Molly bolts. The strongest of anchors, the molly bolt is tapped into a predrilled hole. Once the teeth on the molly have taken hold, the bolt is backed out expanding the legs of the molly behind the wall surface and holding the anchor tightly in place. Some mollys are meant to be tapped through a small guide hole (they have a pointed tip), while others are meant to be driven through a full-sized hole.

Perfect Drilling

On the surface, drilling looks like one of the easiest techniques in the workshop. But there are a lot of ways basic drilling can go wrong. The key is to use the right bit, securely hold the piece being drilled, and drill pilot holes in most cases.

Pilot holes help guide fasteners and, in the case of joining two pieces of wood, pilot holes can protect against splitting or splintering, and may even stop small screw breakage. Predrilling also prevents small, unseen cracks that can lead to joint failure down the road. As a general rule of thumb, a pilot hole should be about equal to the fastener's minor diameter. In the case of a screw,

PILOT HOLE DIMENSIONS FOR COMMON SCREW SIZES	
#6	$3/32$"
#8	$7/64$"
#10	$1/8$"
#12	$5/32$"

that means the diameter of the shaft without the threads. For nails, it means $1/64$ inch less than the diameter of the nail.

As you work on different projects or adapt the designs to create your own, you may need to drill holes to join pieces at unusual angles, to hide fasteners, or make parts of the design adjustable. Jigs and templates can help you do all those things, and basic types of both can be found in most hardware stores. In particular, pocket hole jigs (commonly known by the brand name Kreg) can be a wonderful hardware-store find. Inexpensive and easy to use, these allow you to make a hole and drive a screw through the face and edge of one board at a 45-degree angle, into the face of another board or member of another material (joining perpendicular surfaces). Pin templates are also useful, allowing you to quickly and accurately drill a grid of holes to, for instance, allow a shelf inside a bookcase to be adjusted with dowels or pins.

A – Twist bit (coated)
B – Spur-point bit
C – Brad-point bit
D – Masonry bit
E – Spade bit
F – Ceramic tile bit
G – Twist bit (brass)
H – Twist bit (high-speed steel)
I – Spade bit (metric)
J – Step bit
K – Countersink bit

A   B   C   D   E   F   G   H   I   J   K

THE TOOL AISLE: POWER DRILL SHOPPING GUIDE

Although you can still buy a corded electric power drill, most shoppers opt for a cordless power drill that offers greater convenience and every bit as much power as corded models. Drill technology has advanced quite a bit over the years, and manufacturers now pack a lot of power in a lightweight package, crafting tools that are comfortable to use and get the job done with little fuss or muss. Here are the top factors to keep in mind when considering a new drill.

- **Size.** The first consideration in picking a drill that will meet your DIY needs is size. Power drills come in ½", ⅜"—and, far more rarely, ¼"—sizes. The size simply determines how big a drill bit the drill can accommodate. The ⅜" drill is the most common size for general home use, although you won't go wrong with a ½" drill.

- **Power.** You'll find cordless drills ranging from 6 volts up to monster units boasting 36 volts. Drills rated from 12 to 16 volts are the most common for use by homeowners.

- **Batteries.** You'll want to select a drill with batteries rated for the longest charge and quickest charging time, while still being within your budget. Of course, this isn't a worry if you're opting for an old-school corded model.

- **Speed.** The speed of the drill is rated in rpms, and the faster any drill is, the quicker and more efficiently it will drill. But, of course, that also means the quicker it will drain the battery. Home-use drills rated between 500 and 1,500 rpms are the most common. Choose one based on the type of drilling you anticipate doing; small odd jobs call for a lower rating, but if you're an avid craftsperson who tackles complex projects, go high speed.

- **Weight.** Seem like a non-factor? Wait until you spend the better part of an afternoon drilling joint holes and cabinet peg holes. A heavy drill can wear your arm out and be unpleasant to use. On the same note, check out any drill before you buy it, to ensure the grip suits your hand and the balance seems comfortable to you. Drills last a long, long time and an uncomfortable one will make home projects a lot less pleasant.

Given how far cordless drill technology has come, there are certain must-haves you should seriously consider when shopping for a cordless unit.

- **Autoshift feature.** This handy option automatically sets the speed and torque that is best for the drilling being done, saving battery life, frustration, and poor results.

- **Comprehensive drill package.** In addition to the drill, it's wise to buy one that comes packaged with charger, extra battery, a full set of bits, and a rugged drill carrying case that will hold up to bouncing around in the back of a pickup or the occasional drop onto a garage floor.

- **Lithium-ion batteries.** These are head and shoulders above any other battery for cordless drill use.

Useful Bits

If you're tackling projects like the ones in this book, you will inevitably be dealing with assemblies that combine different materials. The right drill bit can make all the difference in joining those dissimilar pieces securely and quickly.

HSS (High-Speed Steel) bits. These not only make quick work of holes in wood, but they are also excellent at drilling PVC pipe, other types of formed plastic, fiberglass, and soft metals such as aluminum. Titanium-coated HSS bits are even tougher, creating less friction and staying sharper longer than regular HSS bits.

Cobalt bits. The tough nature of cobalt bits make them ideal for drilling even tough metals, like stainless steel or diamond plate.

Carbide-tipped bits. Although these are some of the priciest drill bits, they are also the toughest and can drill not only wood, but masonry as well.

Step bit. Shaped like a terraced cone, these are meant specifically for drilling through thin sheets of metal.

Countersink bits. Adding a polished look to any wood or melamine surface, countersink bits drill both the primary hole and countersink the top of the hole to allow the fastener head to sit flush with surface.

Hole saws. These are used to cut large, perfectly round holes in metal or wood.

Precise Cutting

Fabricating projects from different materials inevitably means cutting those materials to suit your needs and the dimensions of the design. Any hardware store worth its salt offers a range of hand and power tools to do the job.

Handsaw. Handsaws are inexpensive and easy-to-use alternatives to powered saws, but you need to select the right one for the cutting you intend on doing the most (or buy more than one to accommodate different situations). You'll also have to be prepared for a hefty workout, even on small projects. Rip saws are rough-and-tumble options for crude cutting of large pieces. They move quickly and easily through most wood, but tend to leave a very rough edge. They are best used to rip with the grain of the wood. Cross-cut saws cut across the grain of the wood and require more work to make the cut, but also leave a smoother, finer cut edge. Panel or box saws are cross-cut saws meant for finer work (they're shorter than standard cross-cut saws). Back saws have the greatest number of teeth and are consequently intended for fine woodworking.

Handsaw

Hacksaw. The beauty of a hacksaw when dealing with different materials is that you can quickly change the blade to suit the material or the type of cutting you need to do. There are general hacksaw blades, metal-cutting

TOP TIP

You can create a simple drill-bit depth gauge by wrapping the bit with a band of painter's tape at a point that matches the desired hole depth.

blades, fine woodworking blades, and more. The downside is that they can take quite a bit of effort to cut through something like metal, and the handle design can impede access in certain cutting situations.

Hacksaw

Circular saw. The word that epitomizes a circular saw is *versatility*. Fit with the appropriate blade, a circular saw can cut wood, metal, and even masonry. The saw is handheld, which makes it convenient for cutting project materials quickly on site, with little fuss. But used with a jig or guide, a circular saw can also make the long or fine cuts you'd expect to make on a table saw.

Reciprocating saw. This monster is the sledgehammer of saws. A reciprocating saw can make quick work of any wood or metal cutting task. This saw is big and powerful, with a projecting blade that makes its reach impressive. However, reciprocating saws are rarely used for fine work, or where the cut line will be sanded and visible in the finished project. The truth is, for most project work, a reciprocating saw is overkill.

Miter saw. Sometimes called chop saws, miter saws are essentially circular saws mounted on a platform. The mount can be adjusted to hold the saw at an predetermined angle for miters modest to severe. They are fairly portable and are incredibly handy for small-piece cutting—especially

Circular saw

Jigsaw. Perhaps best known as the go-to tool for curved cuts, jigsaws can also be used for straight cuts. However, they won't be as accurate or efficient as a circular saw on straight lines, unless you use a guide and are very careful. Even then, the cuts can be jagged. Like most other powered saws, a jigsaw can be fit with a range of blades available at any well-stocked hardware store, including those meant for cutting stone, ceramics, metal, and plastic.

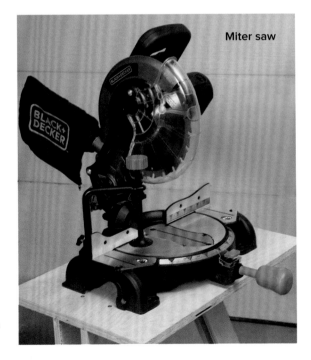

Miter saw

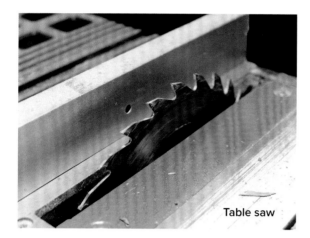

Table saw

The type of saw is just one part of the project fabrication equation. You'll also need to use the right blade to achieve the best cut with the least effort. In general, the number of teeth on any saw blade will determine how fast and clean the blade will cut, and what type of cut it will be capable of making. The more teeth, the finer the cut, with less splintering or other defects. Rip cut blades are meant to make rougher cuts along the length of the wood, and consequently have fewer teeth. Crosscut blades make finer, less aggressive cuts across the grain of the wood and will typically have two or more times the number of teeth that a similar rip cut blade would. (All this holds true whether the blade is cutting plastic, metal, or wood.) Combination blades are a good compromise and an excellent choice for general project work because they can rip and crosscut stock. You can also turn to specialized blades for those moments when you need to get through a bit of sheet metal or a cinderblock.

Diamond blades, sometimes sold as *continuous-cut blades*, are a type of circular blade meant for cutting stone and ceramics. Depending on the individual blade, it may be intended for dry work, wet work, or both.

Turbo blades and *segmented blades* are types of diamond blade (with serrated rim and gulleted rim, respectively). The blades are used for cutting brick and concrete. Although the finished cut won't be as polished, most other blades would have a hard time making it through these materials.

Like diamond blades, *abrasive blades* have a continuous rim rather than individual teeth. The rim is coated with a specialized cutting medium—usually aluminum oxide or silicone carbide—that make these ideal for cutting through metals.

for mitered joints. However, these are not effective for cutting unwieldy pieces, such as a sheet of plastic or sheet metal. Any especially wide piece may be simply impossible to cut with the saw.

Table saw. Table saws can be quick and efficient at cutting project pieces, especially multiples. A table saw does have its limitations, though. Even small table saws can't really be considered portable. Changing blades can be an involved process for cutting plastic or metal, and some sheet goods will be difficult to maneuver on the table. They are also expensive and require a great deal of power.

Choosing a Saw Blade

The number and shape of teeth on a saw blade determine how fine and fast a cut it can make.

Making the Cut

Regardless of the saw and blades you choose, you'll want to make the cleanest cut possible. That starts with precise cut-line marking. The

CUTTING A-ROUND

Depending on the hardware store project you're tackling (or have designed yourself), you may have to cut unusual shapes, such as square or round tubes. Here's an easy way to accurately mark and make clean cuts on continuous shapes like pipe and tubing.

What You Need:

▶ Pipe
▶ Measuring tape
▶ Non-permanent marker or grease pencil
▶ Strip of stiff cardboard
▶ Masking tape

1. Cut a strip of stiff cardboard from a box (the cardboard should be flexible enough to bend into a circle without crimping). The strip should be significantly longer than the diameter of the pipe you're cutting. Make sure that at least one edge of the cardboard is perfectly straight.

2. Wrap the cardboard around the pipe, lining up the straight edge with the cut mark. Overlap the cardboard as much as necessary to make a tight fit. Secure it in place with masking tape.

3. Use a marker or grease pencil to extend the cut mark all the way around the pipe. Make sure the mark is clearly visible and then remove the cardboard. Make the cut with a saw, following the cut mark.

- **Alternative:** If you would like to both mark the tube and create a cutting guide for a circular saw, create a collar from thick cardboard. Mark the cut line as described above, then slide the collar further down the tube to exactly the distance that matches the shoe of your circular saw. Tape the collar in place securely and it will function as a guide for the circular saw cut.

clearer the cut line, the more likely you'll follow it precisely. Use a straightedge and a marker that will visually stand out against the surface of whatever material you're cutting.

Prevent splintering or other defects when cutting wood or concrete by laying down a strip of painter's tape along the proposed cut. Mark the cut line on top of the tape, and score the cut line with a utility knife. Saw right through the tape and the score line for an extremely clean cut.

Cutting Metal

Although you can use a jigsaw or table saw equipped with a metal-cutting blade, it is often quicker to cut thin metal like sheet metal with tin or sheet metal snips, especially if the edge won't be visible in the completed construction. You can also use a hacksaw, although the dimensions of the hacksaw limit the depth of material to which it can follow a cut line. In any case, always smooth the cut edge because it will inevitably be sharp enough to cause injury. A file is a great way to round over a cut metal edge.

Expanded sheet is a handy material that can be a challenge to cut. Although you can use snips of one sort or another, a right-angle grinder with a thin blade will make short work of an expanded sheet cut.

Plumbing pipe, like the pipe used in the Utility Organizer on page 30, is traditionally cut with a snap cutter, a plumbing tool that makes accurate, clean cuts in any pipe. The problem is, snap cutters can be expensive. Most home DIYers rent snap cutters when necessary. Many people, however, use reciprocating saws with a diamond blade in place of a snap cutter. A powerful reciprocating saw can cut quickly through pipe, but it can be hard to control, leaving a slightly uneven cut line. If you feel comfortable handling an angle grinder, use a diamond blade to cut quickly through even thick plumbing pipe (although it can be hard to see the cut line clearly, so you need a good sense of how to cut straight). Hacksaws provide exceptional control, but translate to a lot of time, effort, and expense, because you'll most likely have to change blades before you're done with even a single pipe cut. Choose the method that works best for you, your time, your effort, and your budget.

Precise Measuring

No matter what material the project calls for, correct measurements are going to be key to how good the completed construction looks, and how stable and usable it is. Many of the projects in this book, or any built-in project you tackle, will involve two types of measurement: the dimensions of the project itself and measuring the space into which it will be installed.

Although you can follow the directions and measurements for any project in the book exactly as they're given, you may want to adapt the design of a project like the Custom Laundry Center on page 114 to your own preferences or spaces. Be careful when you customize a project; measurements such as lumber and pipes are not always what they seem—or what they are labeled. A standard modern 2 x 4 is not actually 2 inches by 4 inches, while a 2-inch pipe will actually have an outside diameter larger than 2 inches.

The secret to altering any project's dimensions is to never change one part or element of the project in isolation. There is typically a domino effect to any change, so you should look at the entire project when altering any measurement.

Tin snips are the simplest—and often the most efficient—way to cut sheet metal.

Whenever you're installing a project, such as the Closet Home Office on page 111, it's essential to accurately measure the space where the project will be installed, to identify stud location and ensure the finished project will fit appropriately. Although you can do this fairly effectively with a tape measure and stud finder, a laser measurer offers a way to make extremely precise measurements easily and quickly. These handy instruments also allow you to measure

NOMINAL LUMBER SIZE VS. ACTUAL SIZE	
1 × 2"	¾ × 1½"
1 × 3"	¾ × 2½"
1 × 4"	¾ × 3½"
1 × 6"	¾ × 5½"
1 × 8"	¾ × 7¼"
2 × 2"	1½ × 1½"
2 × 3"	1½ × 2½"
2 × 4"	1½ × 3½"
2 × 6"	1½ × 5½"
2 × 8"	1½ × 7¼"

areas that may be difficult to measure because of access. Laser measurers range in price from $20 to well over $100, with higher prices indicating more exacting accuracy, durability, and added functionality (such as stud finding, wire detection, or greater range).

GAUGE THICKNESSES (INCHES)

GAUGE	METAL	ALUMINUM
3	0.2391	0.2294
4	0.2242	0.2043
5	0.2092	0.1819
6	0.1943	0.1620
7	0.1793	0.1443
8	0.1644	0.1285
9	0.1495	0.1144
10	0.1345	0.1019
11	0.1196	0.0907
12	0.1046	0.0808
13	0.0897	0.0720
14	0.0747	0.0641
15	0.0673	0.0571
16	0.0598	0.0508
17	0.0538	0.0453
18	0.0478	0.0403
19	0.0359	0.0320
20	0.0359	0.0320

A laser measurer gives extremely accurate readings for locating your project.

sophisticated edge profile on wood and metal. Router bits are available for wood, plastic, and metal cutting, adding to the versatility of the tool. Use a router with a jig and you can create elaborate designs in a wood panel.

Finishing Your Project

Some of the projects in this book, and indeed, many projects created with readymade structures will not need to be painted or stained because the raw materials in their natural state may present the look you want. For instance, if you build a Crown Molding Shelf (page 138), the shelf may not need finishing to fit right in.

In other cases, you'll want to cover up the natural state of the materials you use. That will involve using paint, stain, or a clear finish, depending on the material. No matter what, though, you'll most likely have to do some amount of sanding or smoothing before finishing your creation.

Routing

Although most novice and intermediate home DIYers don't own routers, it's a tool worth considering—especially for project work. Routers let you easily add grooves into edges and faces of project pieces, and allow to you put a

Super Sanding

Picking the right sandpaper is key to prepping the surface of whatever materials you've used in the project. You'll find sandpaper in many different formats to suit different power sanders and hand sanding applications. These include plain sheets, self-adhesive pads (round and rectangular), precut forms, and even belts. Start your finishing by selecting the right tool.

You'll never go wrong sanding by hand. Although it can require a lot more elbow grease, hand sanding also affords you a much greater degree of control. Use a palm or orbital sander for small and medium jobs (either would be appropriate for all the projects in this book). These come with round, square, and pointed pads and allow you to see the surface as you work. Bigger sheet sanders work more quickly and are usually more powerful. Belt sanders use a closed loop of sandpaper and work very quickly, even with fine-grit papers. That means that they can sand a large area quickly, but errors and oversanding can happen in the blink of an eye.

Aside from the sander itself, the paper—and especially the type of abrasive you choose—will be dictated by what you need to sand.

Garnet. This is the traditional natural material used on the most common sandpapers. It wears off quickly, but is a good choice for a range of materials.

A downdraft sanding box directs air through a pegboard top into a shop vacuum and keeps airborne dust from sanding under control.

Emery. Also a natural material, emery is used for metal. Coarser grits can quickly remove rust and even residual paint and markings, while finer grits can be used to polish the surface so that it can be left natural.

SANDING GRITS

GAUGE	APPLICATION
40–60	These are the coarsest grits and consequently used for the crudest sanding, such as roughing up a surface to be smoothed in degrees, removing prior finishes, or shaping plastics or wood.
60–100	This range accounts for most of the general prep work done, such as giving wood or metal a tooth prior to painting, or sanding between coats of a finish.
100–220	This is considered superfine sandpaper meant for finishing work and sanding out minor imperfections in a finish; at the upper end, superfine papers are meant for polishing metal surfaces or working on extremely glossy or high-end finishes on wood. Grits above 220 are exceedingly fine, and those papers are meant for specialized applications, such as polishing fine-machined parts.

Aluminum oxide. This common synthetic is an excellent all-purpose sanding medium that lasts appreciably longer than garnet. It can be used equally well on wood, metal, and plastics. It is most often used with power sanders.

Silicon carbide. Want to get the job done quickly even if the paper doesn't last as long? Turn to this excellent abrasive. Often used in wet sanding applications, silicon carbide is especially good at rough work—removing paint and rust or roughing up a surface between coats of a finish. It is excellent on wood, metal, and plastic.

Zirconia alumina. This is a more modern abrasive that is highly effective and lasts even longer than aluminum oxide. It is primarily used for power sander pads and belts and is efficient at removing rust and paint. It works on metal, wood, and plastics—including troublesome surfaces such as fiberglass.

Ceramic alumina. This is a less-common abrasive that offers all the advantages of zirconia alumina and is primarily used in sanding discs and belts.

The keys to a good finish application, regardless of the product you're using or the sanding you've done, are the following:

Cleanliness. Any dirt, grease, or debris can prevent paint from properly adhering to the surface of metal, wood, plastic, or veneers. Not only should you make sure that obvious dirt and grime are removed from the surface to be painted, you should also take steps to remove contaminants that may be hard to see. That's why it's a good idea to clean smooth surfaces such as plastic, or prefinished wood, with glass cleaner.

Tooth. Any surface you're finishing should be slightly—although not too much—rough. This is called having a "tooth" and allows whatever finish you apply to adhere tightly to the surface. In the case of rougher wood surfaces, providing the appropriate tooth may mean smoothing out the

surface slightly with 80-grit sandpaper. In the case of metal pipe or plastic sheet goods, you'll need to rough up the surface to create any tooth at all.

The right stuff. Key to a great finish on any material is using a product meant for that material. For instance, only a couple of paints are meant specifically for plastic; other types of paint might look good right after application, but they will begin to crack and flake off in short order. Metal also requires specific paints meant for the material, and certain metals may not take paint at all. In most cases, it pays to prime the surface before painting (unless you're applying a stain or clear finish). Manufacturers' labels clearly spell out what materials the product is meant to be used on. That's one of the reasons reading paint and finish labels before applying them is a must.

Special Section: Safety First!

Every aisle in a home center is an unbridled opportunity to discover and build fun and useful creations. But many of those aisles, and the tools and materials they contain, also offer some level of risk if used improperly. That's why work safety should always be the first consideration when you tackle a new project. The most basic expectation you should have for any project you build is to come away from the process uninjured, with a creation that won't harm anybody else. The guidelines below will ensure that happens.

Dress for Success

Your workshop is no place for high fashion. Wear the right gear any time you work on a project and you'll not only make yourself more comfortable, you'll head off nagging minor injuries, avoid major problems like a snagged loose piece of clothing, and perhaps even prevent long-term damage such as hearing loss.

Gloves. Good work gloves are worth their weight in gold. However, there are many different types of work gloves, and it's wise to buy specific

gloves for different activities. For instance, a combination neoprene-cotton glove would be great for gardening, but not so much for general workshop project building. If you're going to be handling sharp tools or cutting metal, get yourself some cut-proof metal mesh gloves. For general workshop use, consider a high-quality leather glove, with reinforced palm and fingers and some sort of lining. They'll not only be comfortable, but they'll provide a lot protection from small nicks and bruises.

Eye safety. Eyes are fragile organs. Even small damage or irritation can cause big problems. That's why a good pair of safety glasses is a must for anyone looking to stay busy in a home workshop. Look for a sturdy frame and polycarbonate lenses with side shields. Check the label; glasses rated for impact resistance (as opposed to simple protection against splashes and dust) carry a "+" after the manufacturer's name. Find a pair that's comfortable, so keeping them on won't be bothersome.

Ear protection. Studies increasingly show that hearing loss can occur after what could easily be considered minimal exposure to loud noises. If you're running a table saw or other power equipment on a regular basis—especially inside the confines of a garage or home workshop—you should invest in some quality ear protection. Basic earbuds or earplugs offer some protection, but if your hearing really matters to you, it's wise to invest a little more in earmuffs specially designed for construction and landscape work.

Dust masks and respirators. One of the most common mistakes home DIYers make when it comes to safety is using a dust mask where a respirator is needed. Simple dust masks are great if you're sanding or otherwise raising a dust cloud. But for vapors or fumes from solvent or petroleum-based finishes, you need a dual-cartridge respirator, with cartridges rated for use with the material you're using.

Clothing. Any time you're working with power tools or manipulating unwieldy or heavy materials, the proper attire can head off injury and make you more comfortable and productive. Whenever possible, wear snug-fitting long-sleeve shirts, which will protect your arms against abrasions and ensure no dangling clothing gets entangled in the moving parts of tools or snagged on sharp corners of materials. Similarly, long pants are usually better than shorts, and snug-fitting long pants are a much better choice than sweats or other baggy clothing. Good work shoes or boots are a must, to keep you steady when maneuvering heavy materials and to protect your feet. Sandals, flip-flops, or open-toed footwear of any kind are not appropriate for working on hardware home projects. Lastly, leave your jewelry, including watches, in the jewelry box; the potential for snagging is just too great.

Best Practices

Most safety practices are a matter of basic common sense. However, many serious workshop accidents occur because someone decided to take a shortcut or do something that flies in the face of commonsense, "just this once." To prevent any injuries or accidents, follow these guidelines:

Never . . .

- remove power tool guards, or force them out of position. Sure, safety guards on tools such as circular saws can get in the way and slow you down. But they can also save your fingers and limbs from serious injury.
- overtighten blade-locking nuts on saws.
- change blades or other power tool parts when the tool is plugged in.
- cut or drill when off balance. If you have to lean out over a project to secure or saw a piece, adjust where you're standing or how the project is positioned.
- carry a power tool by its cord.
- carry tools up a ladder by the handle. Bring them up in a bucket.
- expose tools to severe temperature extremes on a regular basis. Wildly varying temperatures are a great way to ensure malfunction and possibly breakage in your tools. If that happens while you're using one, there's a good chance of injury.

Always . . .

- read the manufacturers' instructions. Part of the allure of a hardware store or home center is all those bright, shiny new tools and the possibilities they offer. There is an almost irresistible compulsion to start playing with your new toy the moment you get home. Fight that compulsion. Manufacturers uniformly provide concise instructions for the safe and sane operation of their tools. That's advice from experts that you can only follow if you actually read it. It only takes a few minutes to read through (not "scan") the material, warnings, and instructions manufacturers provide with their tools. That is some of the most valuable time you'll spend in the workshop.

- unplug tools and power equipment when not in use. Not only are power cords and extension cords tripping hazards, it's far too easy to trigger a power tool when moving it around or bumping it if it is plugged in. The best way to make sure power tools are off is to ensure they are unplugged.

- doublecheck that the power cord for any power tool is nowhere near the cut line when beginning to saw.

- stage. Setting out tools, equipment, and supplies in a logical, clear and tidy way, is a surefire way to guarantee success on any project and avoid injury from tools or materials just lying around in your path of travel. Get in the habit—for projects small and large—of setting aside a clearly demarcated, level surface large enough to organize everything you'll need for the project.

- lift with the knees. Some of the materials in the projects in this book (like prefab cabinets) can be weighty, unwieldy, or both. Back injuries are some of the most common home workshop injuries and most are preventable. Don't bend over to lift; squat instead. And enlist the aid of a helper before you think you'll actually need it.

- keep tools sharp. An old construction-site piece of wisdom is that you'll get hurt quicker by a dull edge than a sharp one. If you don't know how to properly sharpen your own tools, the local hardware store will most likely sharpen them for a very modest fee. In either case, make tool sharpening a semi-annual routine.

- keep a first-aid kit on hand. Fortunately, any well-stocked hardware store—and every large home center—sells complete first-aid kits, so you don't need to assemble one yourself. Just buy it, take it home, and place it somewhere in your work area, where it is clearly visible and accessible.

RUNG UP

Although many of the projects in this book do not require a ladder, no discussion of workshop safety is complete without touching on the issue of proper ladder use. You should always check any ladder before you use it; look for areas of rust or broken parts. Never use a damaged ladder. In addition, ladders sold by hardware stores have a "duty rating"; your weight and the weight of materials and tools on the ladder at any one time should never exceed this rating. You should also follow the "three point rule" whenever you climb a ladder: at least three limbs should always be in contact with the ladder at all times. More general safety guidelines are specific to the two basic types of ladders.

- **Stepladders.** Don't step on the top step (called the "cap" step) and don't use the ladder as an extension ladder when folded up. Always be sure the spreaders are locked when using the ladder.

- **Extension ladders.** Although all ladders require a stable base, it is especially important on the greater heights of an extension ladder; any wobbling or unsteadiness translates to a risky situation. When setting an extension ladder, position it so that the ladder is one foot out from the wall for every four feet of ladder height. Tie off the top of the ladder to prevent the ladder from falling backward, and secure the feet—ideally with a cleat.

Creative Reinventions

The very best storage, furniture, and home design accent options are the ones you can customize for your own space. Building a project to suit allows you to make it look like the rest of your interior, fit exactly the space you've allocated, and capture your style precisely. That's the beauty of the projects in this section. Well, that and their actual beauty.

Although they all look sharp, the projects in this section range from the practical and utilitarian to the nearly whimsical. There really is something for everyone here. The harried mother of three will find a handy way to keep things tidy with the Utility Organizer, while the wine lover will enjoy outfitting his kitchen with the super cool Countertop Wine Rack. In every case, the addition will add style to the home.

As you might expect if you've made it this far in the book, these also represent a variety of skills. The projects in this section will give you a wealth of experience working with different materials, from forming copper pipe into wonderfully eye-catching creations to using standard lumber in surprisingly innovative ways.

Although you may be thinking just in terms of practicality and what you can achieve, this is your chance to challenge yourself a bit. Pick a project that will allow you to learn a new skill or technique, or a new way of working with a material you're entirely familiar with. You can select something for your home, but also keep an eye out for projects that would make good big-occasion, one-of-a-kind presents. Regardless of the project to choose for your next weekend foray, you'll find that one common element runs throughout all of the offerings in this section: fun. Using building materials and hardware store finds in unexpected ways is just a blast. And that may be the best benefit of all.

IN THIS SECTION:

Utility Organizer

In real life, it's not the formal entryway that homeowners worry about. Any space worthy of the title "foyer" pretty much takes care of itself. People politely wipe their feet and come in and out without much fuss, and there's usually a spacious closet that is more than capable of containing any outerwear that might find its way into the house. But the mudroom and other utility spaces? Not so much.

Mudrooms are typically chaotic. They are traditionally back or side entrances that are used much more frequently than a formal front entrance. They earn their name. The room sees tons of traffic and is often ill-equipped to handle that traffic—too small, too little storage, and no space to sit. This can often be the busiest territory in the house and, consequently, it's often the most cluttered and dirtiest space.

It doesn't have to be that way, though. A well-thought-out, well-built organizer can put the whole space right again. It can also be used in just about any utility area, from a workshop to a home office, to help keep things tidy.

The right piece of furniture for the space will be tough as nails, able to withstand the rough and tumble treatment of kids piling in and out of the house. It should also be cleanable, easy to install, and—whenever possible—look sharp. The ideal all-in-one organizer will be a multipurpose piece of furniture. Not only should it keep jackets and other outerwear organized and off the floor, it should have some shelf space for odds and ends like gloves and hats. The best structure will even include a place to sit and pull off galoshes, or set down those awkward bags of groceries or packages you've just retrieved from the post office.

That's exactly how this unit was designed. This simple, three-section framework can be built from just about any sturdy sheet good and can easily be customized to meet your needs, tastes, and décor. Accent the structure with prefab corner shelves, a memory-foam bathmat for the seat, decorative hooks, or other readymade touches that will make it all your own.

WHAT YOU NEED:

MATERIALS

- (1) ¾" × 4 x 8' sheet plywood
- (2) ¼ × ¾ × 96" finger jointed pine screen molding
- 2" self-tapping wood screws
- 3" wood screws
- (3) 36" × 2"-dia. black iron pipe
- (6) 2" black iron flanges
- (4) 3" steel L brackets
- 3 coat hooks
- Wood glue
- Masking tape or painter's tape
- Primer and paint, or stain (optional)

TOOLS

- Circular saw
- Stud finder
- Power drill and bits
- Torpedo level
- 4 level
- Carpenter's pencil
- Measuring tape
- Long metal straightedge
- C-clamps or bar clamps
- Utility knife (optional)
- Palm sander and sandpaper (optional)
- Paintbrush (optional)
- Eye and ear protection
- Work gloves

UTILITY ORGANIZER CUT LIST

KEY	QTY	PART NAME	DIMENSION	MATERIAL
A	1	Seat	¾ × 17⅞ × 29¼"	Plywood
B	1	Leg	¾ × 17⅞ × 15"	Plywood
C	1	Divider	¾ × 18⅝ × 78"	Plywood
D	1	Backer	¾ × 29¼ × 78"	Plywood
E	3	Rods	2"-dia. × 30"	Black pipe
F	1	Divider edge trim	¾ × 78"	Pine
G	1	Backer edge trim	¾ × 78"	Pine
H	1	Seat-front edge trim	¾ × 30"	Pine
I	1	Seat-side edge trim	¾ × 17⅞"	Pine
J	1	Leg edge trim	¾ × 15"	Pine

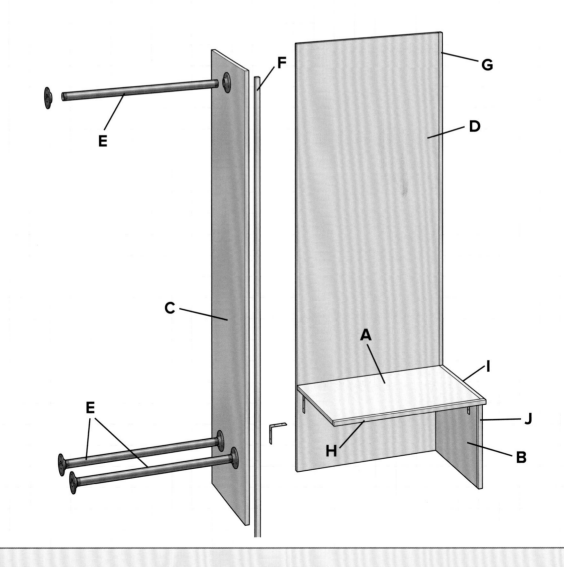

How to Build a Utility Organizer

STEP 1: Measure and mark the plywood sheet for the cuts to make the backer, divider, seat and leg. Use a circular saw fitted with a fine-toothed crosscut blade or similar, and a guide clamped across the sheet. Cover the cut line with masking tape, to avoid splintering. NOTE: When cutting with the circular saw, mark and cut the plywood on the back (bad-looking) side so that the cut line on the finish side will be cleaner. You can also score the cut lines lightly before cutting, which will help prevent splintering.

STEP 2: Cut the plywood sheet along the cut lines, top section first. Make sure the plywood is adequately supported on sawhorses or on a level, stable work surface.

STEP 3: Lightly sand the cut edges as necessary to clean them up. Have the hardware store cut the plumbing pipe into three equal sections and thread each end of each pipe. Clean the newly cut threads and screw a flange onto each end of each pipe section. Adjust the flanges so each section is exactly the same length.

STEP 4: Clamp the back panel to a clean, level work surface. Coat one long edge in wood glue and hold the divider in place, perpendicular to the edge of the back. Measure and mark screw holes down one long edge of the divider. The holes should be spaced evenly every 4" down the edge, with each hole ⅜" in from the edge.

STEP 5: Clamp the backer on the work table, placing wax paper under the edge where it will be joined to the divider. Spread glue along this edge, then set the divider in position, aligning it with the edge of the backer. Fasten the divider to the backer with four 2" self-tapping wood screws.

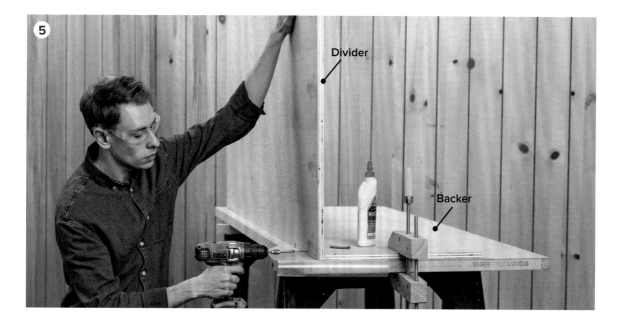

Divider

Backer

STEP 6: Position the unit in the final location. Check that the bars and flanges fit between the divider and the corner wall of the space. Mark the final location of the wood section with key marks on the wall. NOTE: You can tighten or loosen the plumbing flanges to help the bars fit in place, even if the corner wall is not plumb.

STEP 7: Move the wood section and use a stud finder to locate the studs behind where the backer will be attached to the wall. Mark their locations higher than the top of the backer.

STEP 8: Replace the wood section and line it up to the key marks. Position the top hanger rod centered side to side on the divider and about 2" down from the top of the divider and screw the pipe flange to the divider. Check that the bar is level, and mark the screw holes for the flanges on the opposite wall. (Install anchors, if the bar doesn't sit over a stud.) Screw the rod flanges to the wall.

STEP 9: Repeat the process with the two lower shoe rack rods, which should be positioned 8" up from the bottom and 5" in from each edge.

STEP 10: Use a level to line up the stud marks on the backer, and mark locations for screws spaced at the top, middle, and bottom of the backer. Screw the backer to the wall with 3" wood screws every 6 to 8" down the back, along the studs.

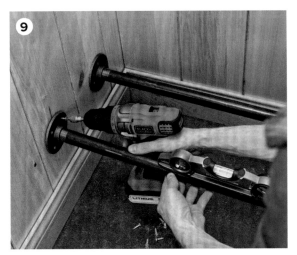

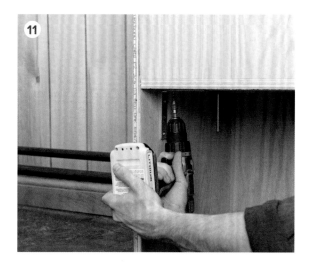

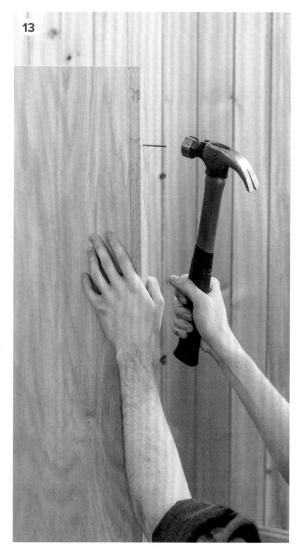

STEP 11: Position one end of the seat on top of the leg, and use a level to position it against the inside face of the divider and the back. Mark the location for the L brackets and remove the seat. Screw the brackets to the divider and then screw the brackets to the seat.

STEP 12: Drill pilot holes down through the top of the seat into the edge of the leg, and screw the seat to the leg.

STEP 13: Lightly sand any edges that might pose a problem on the seat or divider. Finish the exposed edges of the backer, divider, leg and seat with screen molding. Drill pilot holes every 3 to 4" along the molding's length and use finish nails to fasten it in place along the edges.

STEP 14: Prime and paint, or finish the organizer as desired. Measure and mark the placement of the coat hooks on the organizer's back (this project includes three, but you can add more as desired). Screw the hooks in place. Add readymade items such as a memory foam bath mat for the seat or prefab corner shelves to add more storage.

Trim-and-Rope Mat

Will Rogers is credited with saying, "You never get a second chance to make a first impression." Nowhere is that more true than at the front door of your house. Your doorstep is where many visitors are going to form their opinions about the look and style of the house—for better or worse—so why not add a cool decorative (and functional) element that provides a bit of hip to the whole look?

This mat is not big, but it helps enormously with that first impression. It's a very basic construction that is a simple and informal in style. It can be decorated to stand out or colored in subdued tones to blend in. The design combinations are nearly unlimited, because the paracord in the project comes in a range of colors (including some striped styles) and the PVC slats can be colored in several different tones.

Keep in mind that you can alter the basic design to suit your own circumstances. You may want to cut the boards longer, or use more of them to craft a bigger mat for a space like the step outside a busy back door. The surface is nonslip, so this can serve as bathmat (although the mat itself may slip on slick surfaces). In any case, the only potentially challenging part of the project is edge drilling the boards. This process will be much easier, go quicker, and be less prone to errors if you use an edge-drilling jig to guide the drill bit.

WHAT YOU NEED:

MATERIALS

- ▶ (2) 1 × 2" × 8' exterior PVC trim
- ▶ Carpenter's pencil or non-permanent marker
- ▶ 100-grit sandpaper (optional)
- ▶ Masking tape
- ▶ ⁵⁄₃₂" paracord
- ▶ (18) ½ × ½" rubber flat washers

TOOLS

- ▶ Chop saw or table saw
- ▶ Carpenter's square
- ▶ Palm sander
- ▶ Edge-drilling jig (optional)
- ▶ Power drill and bits
- ▶ Scissors
- ▶ Eye and ear protection
- ▶ Work gloves

How to Build a Trim-and-Rope Mat

STEP 1: Use a chop saw or table saw to cut the PVC trim down into ten $2\frac{3}{8} \times 18"$ slats. Use a cutting guide or stop block so the slats for the mat are all exactly the same length.

STEP 2: Use a carpenter's square to stack the slats on edge, perfectly aligned with one another. Measure in from one end 4" and mark all the slat edges for the ¼" rope hole. Repeat at the opposite end of the stakes.

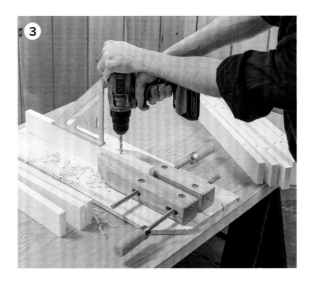

STEP 3: Secure a slat in a vise (or clamped to the work surface) with the marked edge up. If you're using an edge-drilling jig, position it over one mark and drill a ¼" hole all the way through the width of the slat. Repeat at the mark on the opposite end. Drill all the slats in the same way.

STEP 4: Lay out the slats side by side on a flat, level work surface. Wrap the end of the paracord (or rope, if you've opted for that option) with masking tape and guide it through the holes on one end of each stake, weaving the cord through a rubber washer between each stake. Tie the end into a square knot and cut the tail off the knot. Cut the cord on the opposite side, leaving enough cord for a knot, and tie the knot. Repeat the process with the holes at the opposite ends of the stakes. NOTE: If you're concerned about the knots coming untied over time, you can melt the knots slightly with a lighter (although don't attempt this if you're using sisal rope or other natural fiber).

COLORING PVC TRIM

The PVC trim used here is white and, like all PVC, the color runs throughout the material. So you can cut PVC trim and not have to worry about coloring the ends as you would with other prefinished trim boards. However, PVC comes in a limited number of colors—often only white. That means if you want a custom look, you'll need to color the PVC. Plastic spray paint will bond and comes in a wide array of colors, but eventually it may flake off of the PVC surfaces. For more permanent color, follow this hack. Add a small amount of aniline dye (available at craft stores, woodworking stores, and online) to PVC primer. Start with a couple of drops and add until you achieve the color you want. Brush this solution on the PVC trim and let it dry. The

chemicals in the primer dissolve the surface of the PVC temporarily so it can absorb the dye. Because the color change is a chemical reaction rather than an applied layer, it will hold up better underfoot.

Copper Pipe Pot Rack

Pot racks are that ideal combination of distinctive decorative hallmark and super functional organizational feature. A rack like this one announces that the space is a cook's kitchen. It also keeps the cookware you use most frequently conveniently right at hand. You can certainly purchase any number of pot racks at retail, but why bother, when a more compelling and inexpensive rack awaits you down a few aisles of the hardware store?

Copper pipe is the perfect choice for a pot rack. Strong enough to hold a significant number of heavy pans, it is also soft enough to be easily manipulated into the dimensions and shape that best suits your kitchen. The appearance is a natural for any kitchen, because copper has a warm and inviting look.

Although it may seem daunting to craft a structural element from pipe, never fear; working with copper pipe doesn't require a lot of technical expertise. The key concerns are to make secure, stable connections, and affix the rack to the joists so that it won't move under a load. However, if you prefer a swinging rack, you can always forgo the post connections in these instructions and mount the rack by screwing substantial eye bolts into the ceiling joists and hanging the rack by chains and S hooks.

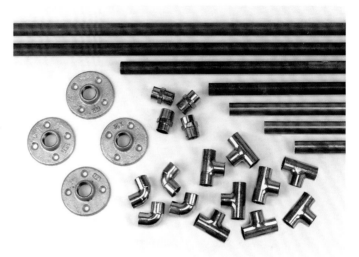

WHAT YOU NEED:

MATERIALS

- 14' × 1" copper tubing
- (8) 1" copper tees
- (4) 1" copper elbows
- (4) 1" cast-iron flanges
- (4) 1" threaded male copper adapters
- Solder
- Soldering flux
- 000 steel wool
- (4) ½" self-tapping metal screws
- (16) #8 wood screws

TOOLS

- Measuring tape
- Marker
- Tubing cutter
- Fitting brush
- Soldering iron or torch
- Flux brush
- Speed square
- Power drill and bits
- Heatproof work gloves
- Eye and ear protection

How to Build a Copper Pipe Pot Rack

STEP 1: Spread the pieces you'll use for the rack on a flat, level work surface. Mark the tubing for cutting, as follows: 4 ends at 9¾"; 8 sides at 8¼"; 2 cross braces at 20"; and 4 posts at 12" (or a different length depending on how high or low you want the rack to hang—which will be affected by the types of pans you want to hang and the height of the users).

STEP 2: Cut all the pipe sections, using a tubing cutter. Set the pipe in the cutter so that the cutting wheel is aligned with the marked cut line. Screw the clamp down to tighten the wheel on the pipe and begin rotating the cutter around the pipe.

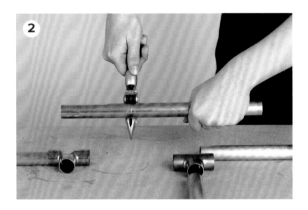

STEP 3: Burnish the cut ends of the pipe sections with 000 steel wool, and burnish the inside of all the fittings with a fitting brush.

Fitting brush

STEP 4: Apply flux around the end of one end section. (The surface must be absolutely clean before you start.) Use the flux brush to spread flux liberally around the pipe end. Slide the pipe into one side of a tee, making sure the two pieces are fully engaged. Heat the soldering iron or light the torch to a blue flame and begin sweating the joint. Move the flame along the joint, back and forth, until it is completely heated, about 30 seconds.

STEP 5: Touch the solder to the pipe. It should melt on contact. Apply the solder evenly to create a uniform bead all the way around the joint. Touch up the soldered joint as necessary, but don't touch the pipe with your bare hands until it has fully cooled. Once the pipe has cooled, burnish the joint with 000 steel wool.

STEP 6: Repeat the process to solder another end section into the opposite side of the tee. Dry fit two elbows to the open ends of the end sections. Working on a flat, level work surface, use a speed square to ensure the open inlet of the tee is perfectly vertical, and that the elbows are perpendicular to the tee. Make key marks on the elbows, remove them, and then flux and solder them in place with the key marks aligned.

STEP 7: Form the sides in the same fashion, soldering the side sections into tees, so that two outside tees are perpendicular to the center tee on each side. Solder one side assembly into an elbow of each end, so that the center tee is perfectly vertical, matching the end center tee.

STEP 8: Solder the two cross braces into the tees on the side that has been soldered to the ends. Finally, solder the opposite side into the elbows and onto the cross braces, with the center tee pointing perfectly vertical.

STEP 9: With the aid of a helper, hold the rack in place where you intend to position it. Raise or lower the rack to the optimum height and adjust the length of the posts as necessary.

STEP 10: Solder the posts into the vertical center tees on the ends and sides of the rack frame. Screw copper male-threaded adapters into the flanges, and screw the opposite ends of the adapters to the top of the posts.

STEP 11: Hold the rack up in the mounting location and mark the flange screw holes on the ceiling along ceiling joists. Drill pilot holes and hang the rack by screwing four wood screws through the flange holes and up into the joists.

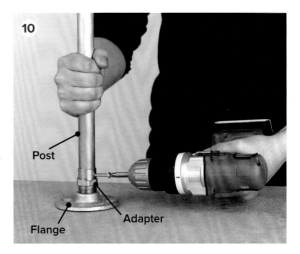

Post
Adapter
Flange

COOL COPPER LOOKS

Right after you complete this rack, the copper surface will look as bright and shiny as a new penny. But a few months later, after exposure to moisture, airborne grease, oils from your hand, and other contaminants, the surface may look dull and dark. That may suit you—and your kitchen's design scheme—just fine. But if it doesn't you can protect and preserve the "like new" look of your copper pot rack by applying a polishing sealer on the surface before you hang it. The sealer will protect the surface over time (although not forever—you'll need to reapply it regularly if you want to keep the surface looking its best). There are many products available and most can be found at—you guessed it—your local hardware store or home center. Just follow the simple instructions on the can or bottle and enjoy a sparkling look for a long time to come.

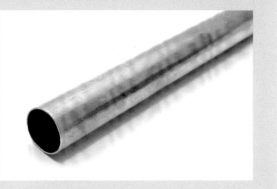

Countertop Wine Rack

A stroll down the lumber aisle offers an amazing number of possibilities, but the some of the best uses for good wood are the simplest. This basic, handsome wine rack is an example of what can be accomplished with a little wood, time, some modest effort, and a few tools.

Although premilled hardwood is specified for this project, you can just as easily use precut hardwood or softwood shelves, as long as they are the right dimensions. Your choice of stain or finish will determine how well the rack complements existing cabinetry and accents in the kitchen—or wherever you decide to place the rack.

The rack as designed accommodates eight wine bottles—from basic red wine to the more uniquely shaped champagne bottles. If you love the rack but find that you want to store and display a large collection of bottles, you can always make a second rack. Sit it next to the first, or drill small holes in the top edge of the ends of one, and matching holes in the bottom of the feet in the second, and pin one on top of the other with skinny dowels.

WHAT YOU NEED

MATERIALS

- ▶ Transfer paper
- ▶ #8 × 1 ¼" wood screws
- ▶ Wood glue
- ▶ Medium- and fine-grit sanding sponges

- ▶ Clear finish or stain
- ▶ 1 × 10 × 24" birch (or similar)
- ▶ 1 × 6 × 48" birch (or similar)
- ▶ ⅜" dowels

TOOLS

- ▶ Circular saw
- ▶ Jigsaw or coping saw
- ▶ Power drill and bits
- ▶ Rubber mallet
- ▶ Bar clamps

- ▶ Paintbrush
- ▶ Router with ¼" roundover bit
- ▶ Eye and ear protection
- ▶ Work gloves

COUNTERTOP WINE RACK CUT LIST

KEY	QTY	PART NAME	DIMENSION	MATERIAL
A	2	Sides	¾ × 9¼ × 10¾"	birch
B	2	Shelf front/back	¾ × 5½ × 20½"	birch

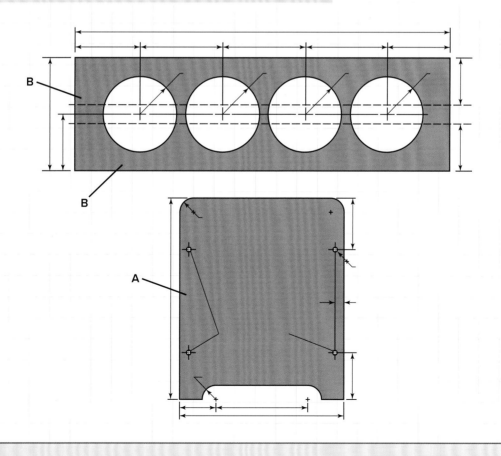

How to Build a Countertop Wine Rack

STEP 1: Cut the wood for the project to match the cut list specifications. Use a copier to enlarge the patterns on page 45. Transfer the rack pattern onto the 1 × 6 wood stock, using transfer paper and a stylus or hard pencil.

STEP 2: Drill a ¼" hole near the edge of each circle, then slip the jigsaw blade into the hole and cut along marked lines to cut out the circles.

STEP 3: Rip-cut each rack piece along the marked line from the pattern, using a circular saw and straightedge guide or a table saw.

STEP 4: Repeat the transfer process with the pieces of 1 × 10 stock, using the pattern on page 45 and marking the screw locations. Cut the wood along the marked lines, using a jigsaw.

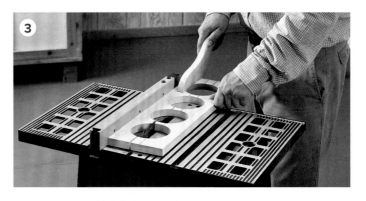

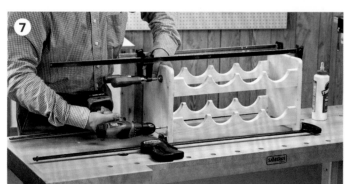

STEP 5: Use a router and a ¼" roundover bit to shape the edges of the panels (except the bottoms of the feet) and the edges of the racks (but not the ends). Sand the faces and edges of all the pieces.

STEP 6: Place the end pieces face-up on a workbench. Drill ⅜" countersunk pilot holes at the marked screw locations. Spread glue on the ends of the rack pieces, assemble the pieces, and clamp the assembly together using bar or pipe clamps.

STEP 7: Drive screws through the pilot holes in the panels and into the rack pieces. Spread glue on the ends of ⅜" dowel plugs or buttons and insert one into each screw hole to conceal the screw heads. Trim and sand the plugs flush after the glue dries.

STEP 8: When the glue is dry, sand the entire unit with a fine-grit sanding sponge and apply two coats of a finish of your choice.

Tasting Table

This compact and handy small table is based on the design used for wine-tasting tables in wineries. They are meant to be out-of-the-way additions to a wine cellar, just big enough to hold a glass of wine and the bottle that fills it. But even if you're not a fan of adult grape juice, you'll find plenty of handy uses for this table. It can hold a lamp and a book alongside your bed, or host a snack right by the couch, as you watch your favorite movie (although you may want to modify the dimensions—specifically the height—to suit your particular use).

The table's supporting structure is made from SPF wood, a softwood lumber product made from spruce, pine, and fir. The wood is cheap but strong, and takes stains and finishes well. To complete the table, you'll need an MDF disc and a little hardware. The result, however, is far more visually powerful than the sum of its parts.

Don't be surprised if you fall in love with this table; not only is it easy to construct, but you can also put it together for a fraction of what a prefabricated table would run you. You might want to plan on making two tables at the same time, because a pair of these is the perfect, balanced complement to a living room suite, or as twins on either side of a bed.

WHAT YOU NEED

MATERIALS

- Black 1½" hex head screws
- Lag screws
- 8d finish nails
- Wood glue
- Stain, paint, or other finish

- ⅛ × 1½ × 75½" strap iron
- (4) 2 × 4" × 8' SPF
- (2) 1 × 4" × 8' pine
- Half sheet ¾" MDF
- 3" wood screws

- 2½" wood screws
- Flat washers
- 1¼" brass wood screws
- Cutting oil
- Black enamel paint

TOOLS

- Table saw
- Jigsaw or bandsaw
- Compass or trammel points
- Belt sander or palm sander

- Drill press (optional)
- Drill and bits
- Hacksaw
- Nut driver

- Clamps
- Paintbrush
- Eye and ear protection
- Work gloves

TASTING TABLE CUT LIST

KEY	QTY	PART NAME	DIMENSION	MATERIAL
A	16	Tabletop	¾ × 2½ × 24"	SPF
B	3	Shelf disc	¾ × 21" dia.	MDF
C	4	Leg	¾ × 3½ × 35½"	SPF
D	4	Filler-short	¾ × 3½ × 10"	SPF
E	4	Filler-long	¾ × 3½ × 23¼"	SPF
F	3	Stemware rack	¾ × 1½ × 12"	Oak

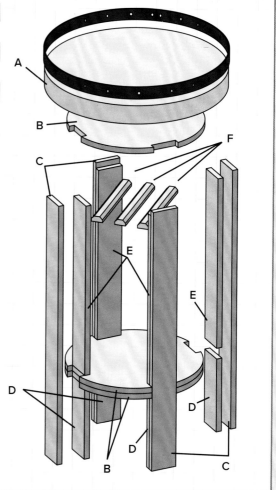

How to Build a Tasting Table

STEP 1: Rip the four 2 × 4s to 2 ½" wide, removing the rounded eased edges. Cut them to length and lay the 16 workpieces on edge and face-to-face on a flat surface. They should be aligned, forming a 24" square. Apply liberal amounts of wood glue to the faces and clamp the pieces together with pipe or bar clamps. Let cure overnight.

STEP 2: Use a compass or trammel points to scribe a 24"-dia. circle on top of the glued pieces.

STEP 3: Cut out the circle using a bandsaw or a jigsaw with a wide, stiff wood-cutting blade. Cut just outside the cutting line so you can sand the edge up to the line.

STEP 4: Lightly resurface the tabletop with a belt sander and 150-grit sanding belt. This will get rid of dried glue squeeze-out and create a smoother, more even surface. Finish-sand the edges.

STEP 5: Apply a coat of thinned shellac to the completely sanded tabletop as a sanding sealer. Let the sealer dry and then stain the tabletop with a dark wood stain, such as dark walnut or the finish you desire. Apply a penetrating topcoat if desired (such as tung oil).

STEP 6: Drill a screw hole every 4" in the metal strap. Use a drill press if possible and lubricate the drilling area with cutting oil. Paint the strap with black enamel.

STEP 7: Center the strap on the edge of the tabletop and mark a pilot hole for the first screw in the middle of the strap. Drive a hex-head screw to fasten the strap. Add the next screw in line, and then the next on the opposite side. Alternate back and forth, bending the strap as you go so it is flush against the wood.

STEP 8: Fabricate the legs by face-gluing the filler strips onto the inside faces of the full-length legs, creating a ¾" recess at the top and a 1½" recess starting 10" up from the bottom. Lay out the legs in a row to ensure that they're even, and attach the filler strips with glue and finish nails.

STEP 9: Cut three 21"-dia. shelves from the MDF. Use the same compass technique you used on the top. Once all three circles are cut, gang them together and sand them so the edges are round, smooth, and uniform.

STEP 10: With the three shelves stacked, divide the top circle into four equal quadrants. Lay a scrap piece of 1 × 4 along one quadrant line, centered side to side on the line. Mark the leg notches on the edge of the circle. Stand the scrap piece on end between the marks and trace the outline of the leg notch on each end of the line. Repeat with the opposite quadrant line to mark all four leg notches.

STEP 11: Cut out the notches in all three shelves with a jigsaw or bandsaw. Sand the notches and square. Separate the three shelves, and fill any nail or screw holes you may have created by ganging the parts.

STEP 12: Drill countersunk pilot holes for 3" wood screws through the legs and into the shelf disc notches. Glue and screw the legs to the shelves. Check that the base is level and square before covering the screw heads with wood plugs or wood filler.

STEP 13: Sand the legs and the shelves and apply your desired finish. Here, the same finish that's applied to the tabletop is applied to both the legs and the shelves (a sealer coat of thinned shellac followed by dark walnut stain and then penetrating oil). Because the stain is dark, the MDF shelves accept it well and blend with the legs and tabletop. But you may prefer to paint the shelves gloss black or even a metallic tone.

STEP 14: Set the tabletop good-side down on a flat surface. Position the base upside down on the underside of the tabletop. Center the base so that the top overhangs equally on all sides. Drill several ¼" access holes through the top shelf, but not into the tabletop. Drill pilot holes into the underside of the tabletop, matching the access holes. Slip metal washers onto 2½" wood screws and drive one at each hole (this washer-and-guide hole system allows for some wood movement).

STEP 15: Cut a 45° bevel on each edge of a 1 × 2" strip of hardwood. Cut the strip into three 12" lengths.

STEP 16: Arrange the three strips parallel to one another on the underside of the top shelf. (Use a wine glass base as a reference for spacing the strips.) With the strips aligned end to end, screw them to the top shelf with countersunk 1¼" brass wood screws.

Rolling Bar Cart

A bar cart is a truly elegant extravagance in any dining room or home. Imagine whipping up a martini or three after a long day at work, or hustling children back and forth. Or think about the look on your friends' faces when you wheel out the cart to serve some refreshments at your next cocktail party. Unfortunately, this is one piece of furniture most people would never think of buying for themselves. No problem. Why buy, when you can make yourself a totally cool version like the one in this project?

This mixologist's assistant features a rough, dark appearance that is meant to stand out against the sparkle of bar and stemware and bottles of wine and alcohol. Although the look is distinctive and industrial, the cart actually fits into a wide range of interior design styles. Of course, you can always switch up the visual by painting the angle irons white or black, and painting the "shelves" in your favorite bold color.

In use, the cart is equally accommodating. If you decide that a bar cart is simply unnecessary for the type of entertaining you do, or is out of place in your kid-oriented home, you can always repurpose this as a mobile kitchen island. You'll find the shape lends itself well to providing a useful work surface, but in just the right shape so as not to interfere with kitchen foot traffic. The rugged durability of the design and construction means that this particular cart can roll up its sleeves and get busy outside the home as well. You can even put it to work in your garage or workshop as a tool or material caddy, or an all-purpose movable work surface.

No matter where you put it, you won't have to worry about day-to-day abuse, water rings, or other dings and dents because they will only add character to the cart.

WHAT YOU NEED

MATERIALS

- (1) 1 ½ × 96" aluminum angle
- (1) ⅝ × 16 × 72" pine panel
- (2) 1 ½ × 13" brushed aluminum cabinet door pulls
- ¼ × 1" lag screws
- (4) 3" casters (2 swivel, 2 rigid)

- #14 × 1" roundhead wood screws
- #12 × ¾" roundhead screws
- 100-grit sandpaper
- Stain or finish

TOOLS

- Jigsaw (or hacksaw), with metal-cutting blade
- Power drill and bits
- ¼" box wrench

- Paintbrush or rag for staining
- Eye and ear protection
- Work gloves

ROLLING BAR CART CUT LIST

KEY	QTY	PART NAME	DIMENSION	MATERIAL
A	3	Shelf	⅝ × 16 × 24"	Pine panel
B	4	Leg	⅛ × 1½" × 24	Aluminum angle
C	2	Pull	1½ × 13"	Brushed aluminum

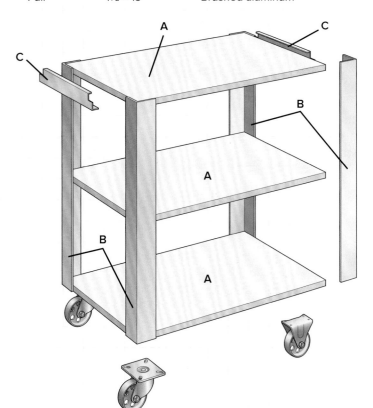

How to Build a Rolling Bar Cart

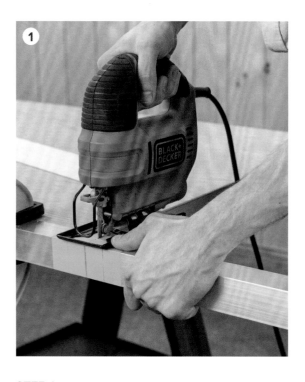

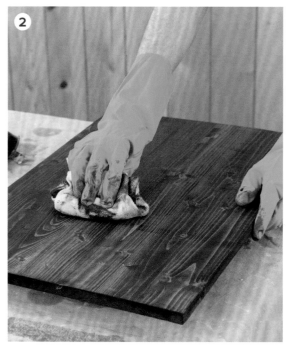

STEP 1: Use a jigsaw with a metal cutting blade to cut the aluminum angle into four equal legs (each slightly less than 24"). Use masking tape over the cut line to prevent the metal jigsaw shoe from scratching the aluminum.

STEP 2: Cut the shelves to size, out of the pine panel. Sand and stain the boards with a dark stain or your preferred finish. For a more worn look, distress the surface before (and even after) staining.

STEP 3: Position an aluminum angle leg along one edge of a sacrificial piece of wood and drill three ¼" holes: one at each end, ⅜" in from the end, and one centered along the length of the leg. Drill the opposite face in the same way, and then repeat with the three remaining legs.

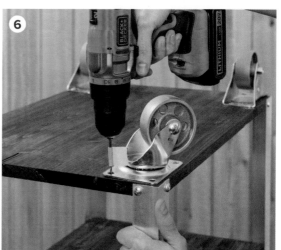

STEP 4: Working on a flat, level work surface, clamp the three shelves standing on edge, parallel, between two legs on either side of the shelves. Mark the edge of the shelves through the leg holes. Drill pilot holes at the marks and screw the legs to the shelves with 1¼" screws.

STEP 5: Stand the cart assembly upright on the work surface and clamp it to the work surface. Check for level and plumb, and then screw the legs to the shelves on the faces that were face-down on the work surface.

STEP 6: Set the cart top-down on the work surface. Position a caster flush to one corner of the cart, and drill pilot holes for the #12 × ¾" roundhead screws. Use a depth gauge marked at ⅝" on the drill bit to prevent drilling all the way through the shelf. Be sure to put the two swivel casters at one end (along a short side) of the bar cart.

STEP 7: Turn the cart right side up, and screw the handles in place along both short edges, by drilling pilot holes through the bottom leg of the handles up into the underside of the top shelf (using a depth gauge) and screwing the handle to the shelf.

Angle Grinder Shopping Guide

An angle grinder is a multipurpose tool that you won't know you needed until you start actually using one in your workshop or garage. Then you won't be able to put it down. Versatility is what angle grinders are all about. Despite the name, this project animal can quickly cut, sand, polish, grind, and even sharpen other tools. Need to customize a tile to fit around an odd-shaped projection in your new bathroom floor? Look no further. Want to carve through that rebar for your addition foundation like a knife through butter? Got you covered. Any angle grinder is easy to handle but will have more than enough power to handle just about any task you can throw its way.

The most common angle grinder used by home craftspeople is a 4½" corded model (although more and more cordless grinders are available). Finding the perfect angle grinder for your projects and the workshop challenges you most often face is a matter of looking at the specs and narrowing down your search by the power and extras you need . . . and those you don't. As with some other handheld power tools, it's a great idea to rent an angle grinder to get a sense of the qualities and key features that will serve you best.

- **Speed.** Angle grinder efficiency is largely determined by the speed at which the wheel turns. Speed ratings are "no-load" measurements—the speed of the wheel turning freely, not held against any surface. Faster is not necessarily better. Although you want a lot of speed if you're going to be grinding down welds or doing a lot of steel work, a slower grinder will be easier to control for finer jobs like sanding and will produce less heat while working. Home-use grinders range in speed from 8,000 to 12,000 rpm. However, you gain even more control by spending a bit more for an adjustable speed grinder; that way, you can tailor the speed to the work you're doing.

- **Safety features.** Although features like wheel and side guards are standard pieces on any angle grinder, a terrific safety option you may want to consider—and not standard on many grinders meant for home use—is a safety slip clutch. This is more important the more powerful your grinder is; the device prevents kickback when operating the grinder. Kickback is not just a jarring annoyance; it can cause serious accidents and injury. You can also pay a little extra for adjustable guards that will allow you greater access with the grinder wheel without sacrificing safety.

- **Ergonomics.** Operation of an angle grinder requires that you be able to position it properly for the job at hand, and that you can leverage your body angle and weight when necessary. That means your hands should fit comfortably on the handle and body of the grinder. But you should also consider the weight of the grinder. If your grip strength is modest, you may want to look at models that are not only lighter, but also thinner. Handle options are a big plus. Common extras include adjustable side handles and vibration-reducing handle grips.

- **Extras.** It's always good to consider your suite of tools when buying any individual addition to your toolbox. If you're buying a cordless angle grinder, you'll find that many manufacturers offer batteries that are swappable between different cordless power tools in their line. That can be a huge plus on a project that requires you to use a drill, grinder, and saw. Quick-change mechanisms can save a lot of time if you regularly switch between wheels for different functions or materials. Most of these allow you to change the wheel without a tool.

Angle Grinder Safety

Wear eye protection, ear protection, and heavy work gloves when operating an angle grinder. If you're working on metal or loose mortar, it also makes sense to wear heavy work shoes. In any situation where you'll be grinding metal or rust, wear a dust mask.

Unplug or remove the battery whenever you change a grinder's wheel.

Orient yourself and the grinder to the work surface so that debris is directed down and away from you.

Secure the work piece so it doesn't move.

Run a new grinding wheel for one minute in a secure area before actually using it, to ensure it is not defective and that it is mounted correctly.

Chunky Club Chair

Sometimes, you just have to make a statement with a piece of living room furniture. It might be that elegant camel-back couch in blue velvet, or a sleek, white, mirror finish credenza that cements the modern-style cred of your home. Or, it might be that you want something assertive, strong, and . . . well, big and chunky. That's when you turn to this chair.

The style is large, rough-hewn, and unmistakably male. The chair will work best when placed in a room with other untamed, natural materials, such as a fieldstone fireplace or the unfinished iron hardware and wide planks of a sliding barn door. Because it's constructed of treated pine, it can also do duty as an outdoor chair, and would be wonderful as one of a pair on a patio. No matter where you put it, give the chair a little space around it to be seen. This distinctive seating will stand all on its own.

As substantial as it might appear, the construction is really rather simple. It goes together quickly courtesy of a few stair tread hangers and easy-to-find lumber. The seat is rather low slung but extremely comfortable. It's the perfect place to spend the better part of an evening reading your favorite novel or just pondering a roaring fire pit. The materials for the chair were purposely selected for customization. You can smooth all the wood and paint or finish it in a chic, more polished, or distress it and take it outside as a showpiece for your deck or patio.

WHAT YOU NEED

MATERIALS

- ▶ (3) 4 × 4 × 96" wood posts (cedar or similar)
- ▶ (1) 2 × 12 × 72" pine
- ▶ 1 upholstered deep seat patio chair cushion with back

- ▶ (24) 6" self-tapping lag screws (GRK type)
- ▶ 1¼" self-tapping wood screws
- ▶ 3" self-tapping wood screws

- ▶ (2) 1½ × 10" stair tread angles
- ▶ (4) 7" stair brackets
- ▶ Paint or stain (optional)

TOOLS

- ▶ Measuring tape
- ▶ Carpenter's pencil
- ▶ Bar clamps or C clamps
- ▶ Miter saw

- ▶ Circular saw
- ▶ Power drill and bits
- ▶ Speed square
- ▶ Paintbrush (optional)

- ▶ Eye and ear protection
- ▶ Work gloves

CHUNKY CLUB CHAIR CUT LIST

KEY	QTY	PART NAME	DIMENSION	MATERIAL
A	12	Sides	3½ x 3½ x 24"	Treated pine (or cedar)
B	2	Seat boards	1½ x 11¼ x 22½"	Treated pine (or cedar)
C	1	Back rest	1½ x 11¼ x 22"	Treated pine (or cedar)

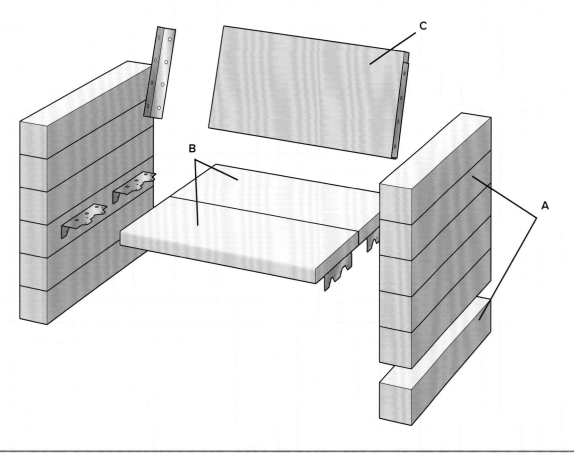

How to Build a Chunky Club Chair

STEP 1: Measure the seat cushions you want to use and doublecheck that the chair measurements suit the cushions. Cut all the leg timbers (inset) to exactly the same dimensions as listed in the cutting list. Cut the 2 × 12s for seat and back using a circular saw. Screw a long piece of 1 × 2 to the fence of your saw through the holes in the back. Screw a stop block to the 1 × 2 to cut all the 4 × 4s to length.

STEP 2: Sand all the 4 × 4s and round over the edges. Build one side by positioning a side timber flush against a stop that has been clamped perpendicular to the edge of the work surface. Sit the next timber for the side flush with the first, and drill countersunk ¼" pilot holes spaced in about 4" from each end, from the bottom of the second timber up into the first. Drive 6" lag screws up through the holes. Continue building the side by adding four subsequent timbers, drilling the lag screw holes offset of the timbers above. Repeat the process with the opposite side.

STEP 3: Determine your preferred seating height by measuring a comfortable chair in your house. Lay each side assembly with its least attractive face up. Position two stair brackets with the L-bend in the bracket aligned with the bottom of the third timber from either end (or to whatever height makes most sense for your preferences). The brackets should be 3" in from either side. Make sure the two sides are mirror images of each other. Screw them in place with 3" wood screws. Repeat with the opposite side.

STEP 4: Stand the sides up, parallel to one another and on edge (the stair brackets will be perpendicular to the work surface or the floor). Position one 2 × 12 seat board between the sides, snug to the bottom stair brackets. Make sure the inside faces of the sides are snug to the seat board edges and screw the brackets to the seat board with 1¼" wood screws. Repeat with the second seat board and second pair of brackets.

STEP 5: Sit the chair upright. Measure up 3" from the seat on one side, at what will be the back of the chair. Position a scrap reference block with the top edge on the line, and use a speed square to adjust the block to a 25° angle slanting backwards. Clamp the reference block in place. Repeat on the opposite side, and then use 3" wood screws to fasten a stair tread angle in place with the bottom resting on top of the reference block. Repeat on the opposite side.

STEP 6: Clamp the back rest in place between the stair tread angles on either side, with the bottom of the back rest aligned with the bottom of the angles. Screw the angles to the back rest with 1¼" wood screws.

QUICK TIP

Design Mods

Want to kick up the cool factor of this chair? Substitute the 4 × 4s with reclaimed antique timbers. More and more retailers are offering lumber salvaged from old factories, barns, shipping containers, and other dilapidated structures. Although you have to be aware that the lumber is usually actual measurements rather than nominal sizes (and the occasional piece may even be unusual, one-off dimensions), with a little searching, you can often find visually interesting lumber that may actually cost less than buying new. Some species of reclaimed lumber are no longer available and added to environmental effects—such as the smoke from tobacco curing barns—that translates to one-of-kind looks you can buy or replicate.

Maple Molding Room Divider

Divider screens are an often overlooked but interesting piece of furniture that adds a lot to any room's layout. It's not hard to find one at retail, but they unfortunately tend toward the bland. If you want a real showstopper, you have to build your own.

This project describes the crafting of a privacy screen with a traditional three-panel design. The panels stand accordion-style, creating a stable structure that is less likely to fall when bumped. This screen is substantial but still lightweight enough to making moving it when necessary a reasonable task for any able adult.

This one, like any privacy screen, can play both a pragmatic and aesthetic role in your interior design. A privacy screen is excellent for visually dividing long narrow rooms into smaller, more visually pleasing, inviting spaces. It can also cordon off a section of a larger room, creating a more intimate conversational nook. Of course, as the name implies, a privacy screen can also be used to provide a modicum of privacy, such as creating a discrete dressing area in a studio apartment.

Ultimately, though, any practical application also involves the decorative potential of the screen. The graphic style of this screen is pure contemporary style, understated, and elegant. It is visually light, thanks to the maple trim used to build the frame. The diffuser panels used at the tops of the frames allow light but block view, making them perfect for an interior privacy screen. You'll find different patterns of diffuser panels—choose the one that suits your tastes (you can even find colored panels online). If you were willing to work with a more finicky material, you could even substitute stained glass for the diffuser panels.

The rest of the construction is fairly straightforward; the bottom of each frame incorporates maple cabinet doors and all the elements are widely available at any well-stocked home center or lumberyard. The maple looks great unfinished, but if you would prefer a different look, paint, stain, or finish the wood components prior to constructing the screen panels.

WHAT YOU NEED:

MATERIALS

Frame Precut Trim Moldings:
▶ (7) $^{11}/_{16}$ × 1½ × 96" (maple)
▶ (10) ½ × ¾ × 96" (maple)

Finish Elements:
▶ (3) ¾ × 16 × 21½" cabinet doors (maple)
▶ (3) $^1/_{16}$ × 24 × 48" light diffuser panels
▶ (4) 4" bifold door hinges
▶ #8 × 1½" GRK screws
▶ 1" brads
▶ Clear silicone adhesive

TOOLS

▶ Measuring tape
▶ Miter saw
▶ Power drill and bits
▶ Claw hammer
▶ Utility knife
▶ Bar clamps
▶ Metal straightedge
▶ Caulk gun
▶ Eye and ear protection
▶ Work gloves

MAPLE MOLDING ROOM DIVIDER CUT LIST

KEY	QTY	PART NAME	DIMENSION	MATERIAL
A	6	Uprights	$^{11}\!/_{16} \times 1\!\frac{1}{2} \times 64"$	Maple
B	9	Rails	$^{11}\!/_{16} \times 1\!\frac{1}{2} \times 21\!\frac{1}{2}"$	Maple
C	12	Horizontal retainer	$\frac{1}{2} \times \frac{3}{4} \times 21\!\frac{1}{2}"$	Maple
D	18	Vertical retainer	$\frac{1}{2} \times \frac{3}{4} \times 11\!\frac{9}{16}"$	Maple
E	3	Diffuser Lite	$^{1}\!/_{16} \times 21 \times 38"$	Maple

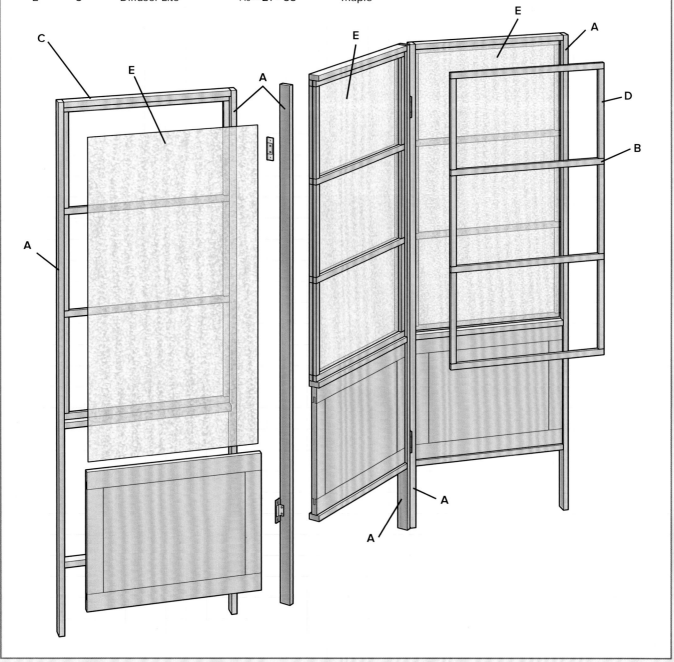

How to Build a Maple Molding Room Divider

STEP 1: Cut all the uprights, rails, and retainers for all three panels before beginning. Stage the pieces so that you can be sure you have all the parts necessary to construct the panels, and that they are uniform, panel to panel.

STEP 2: Measure and mark two uprights 8" up from the bottom, and 17½" up from that mark, make a second mark. Glue three rails between the dividers: one at the unmarked end; one with its bottom face aligned with the 8" mark; and one with it's bottom face aligned with the 17½" mark. (The rails should all be positioned on edge, to match the width of the uprights.) Clamp the rails between the uprights. Use a carpenter's square to ensure the frame is square, and then drill pilot holes through the outside of the uprights into the center of each rail end. Screw the uprights to the rails with two 1½" self-tapping screws per rail.

STEP 3: Cut ³⁄₁₆"-thick shims. Starting at the rail second from the bottom, dry fit a horizontal retainer between the two uprights, butted to the rail and resting on the shims. Drill pilot holes and nail the retainer in place (nail through the ½" side). Use the vertical retainers as spacers for the horizontal retainers. Nail the top retainer in place in the same way. Fasten the horizontal retainers with 1¼" self-tapping screws, driven through pilot holes from the outside of the uprights into the center of the retainers.

STEP 4: Starting from the fastened horizontal retainer, shim the vertical retainers on either side and drill pilot holes into the uprights. Nail the vertical retainers in place, snug to the horizontal retainer. Repeat with this pattern, screwing the uprights to each horizontal retainer and nailing each subsequent pair of vertical retainers in place. This will create an inner frame for the diffuser panel.

STEP 5: Cut the diffuser panel to the dimensions in the cutting list (working on the smooth side, if there is one). The panel here was measured, marked, and a straightedge clamped along the cut line; the panel was then cut with a new utility knife blade by scoring through it about ten times and snapped off. However, depending on the panel you buy, you may need to use a saw for a clean, straight cut. Use masking tape along the cut line and raise the blade of the table saw as high as possible. Work very slowly and wear gloves and eye protection.

STEP 6: Lay a bead of clear silicone adhesive along the inside edge of the interior frame. Lay the textured side of the diffuser panel in the bead of silicone adhesive (inset).

STEP 7: Build the second diffuser panel frame on top of the diffuser panel, fastening the members in the same way and same location as the bottom frame. Be sure the members hold the panel snugly.

STEP 8: Place ⅜"-thick shims at the corners of the square opening in the divider panel (the cabinet door should be centered, front to back, in the opening). Sit the door in the opening and measure to make sure the inset is the same on all four sides. Drill pilot holes through the uprights into the edge of the door, and screw the door in place with 2½" self-tapping screws.

STEP 9: Build the two remaining screen panels in the same manner. Make marks for the hinge on the first panel 7" from the top and 10" from the bottom. Screw the first hinge leaf in place, then set the center panel next to hinge side. Place the panels mirror-image style, so textured side is facing textured side (or smooth to smooth). Align the ends and hold the two panels together, separated by the thickness of the hinge knuckle, and screw the second leaf in place.

STEP 10: Stand the two panels up, then mark and install the hinges for the third panel. Remember to have all the textured sides facing the same way. The knuckles of the second set of hinges should be on the opposite edge of the frame if you want your divider to fold in an S shape. If you would rather have the divider fold in a C shape, fasten the hinges on the same side.

Aluminum Sheet Lamp

Beautiful table lamps can be the jewelry of a home's interior design. A unique table lamp is a wonderful accent, and this project is a prime example. The design is distinctive, original, and sophisticated. It ensures that the lamp can serve as both a source of illumination and a decorative flourish in and of itself.

This lamp is adaptable to different areas. It could go equally well on a bedside table or a living room end table. Keep in mind, though, that it is meant as accent lighting rather than task lighting; it shouldn't be used as a reading or work light. Wherever you place it, it will be extremely convenient thanks to the in-cord switch.

The aluminum sheet used for the body of the lamp is an engaging and fascinating material. It's stiff enough to hold its shape over time, but pliable enough to bend to just about any angle or curve. The sheet comes in several different cutout designs; this project uses a product with a diamond cut, but you'll find surface patterns from highly complex and beautiful Fleur-de-lis, to simpler, less fussy looks such as a basic geometric pattern.

This particular lamp project uses an all-in-one cord-and-socket unit. This is specified to avoid any wiring that might intimidate novice DIYers. But if you're willing to do very basic and simple electrical work (wiring two wires from a cord to the socket), you open up your options. For instance, you could pair a brass socket with a white cord, or a use a nickel-finish socket that would blend more seamlessly with the aluminum sheet. Regardless, never exceed the maximum wattage for which the socket and cord are rated in the bulb you use. And be aware that the metal surface can heat up even with a modest bulb—so keeping the lamp out of reach of pets and young children is a wise idea.

WHAT YOU NEED:

MATERIALS

- ¼" plywood
- 1 × 1 × 24" pine
- Black hanging lamp light cord with socket
- (2) cable clamps
- 40-watt bulb
- 12 × 24" patterned aluminum sheet
- ¾" flathead wood screws
- 1¼" flathead wood screws
- 80-grit sandpaper
- Primer and white gloss acrylic paint

TOOLS

- Measuring tape
- Pencil compass
- Marker
- Carpenter's pencil
- Power drill and bits
- 1" spade bit
- Jigsaw
- Bar clamps
- Tin snips
- Paintbrush
- Eye and ear protection
- Work gloves

ALUMINUM SHEET LAMP CUT LIST

KEY	QTY	PART NAME	DIMENSION	MATERIAL
A	3	Disks	¼ × 6"-dia.	Plywood
B	2	Posts	¾ × ¾ × 9¾"	Pine

QUICK TIP

Lamp Options

There are many, many different ways to go with this lamp to customize it and put your own signature on the design.

- **Size.** Aluminum is typically sold in finished sheets that are either 24" × 36" or 36" square. Create a much taller lamp—essentially a floor lamp—by using the full width of the sheet and otherwise following this project's instructions. You will, however, have to weight the base with metal inserts, or other modifications to ensure the lamp doesn't fall over when bumped.

- **Change the type.** A table lamp is a lovely accent unless you have no spare tabletop space on which to put the lamp. In that case, you can consider modifying this project into a hanging lamp or sconce. For a sconce, use a divider piece of wood running the entire seam, instead of the base. You'll need to cut a channel in the back of the wood for the cord and a hole for the socket. To hang this lamp, use only the top disk of the base; the cord can be trailed out the top and down to an outlet, or up to a plug socket in a ceiling box.

- **Material.** Aluminum isn't the only sheet metal that is stamped with surface cutout designs. You can find variations in brass, which would make an even more attention-grabbing light fixture. The project instructions would otherwise be exactly the same.

How to Build an Aluminum Sheet Lamp

STEP 1: Clamp a plywood sheet across two sawhorses. Use a carpenter's pencil compass to mark three 6" circles. Use the compass to mark two of the circles with a 4" circle inside the outer circle. Cut out the circles—and the inner circles— by drilling an access hole and then using a jigsaw.

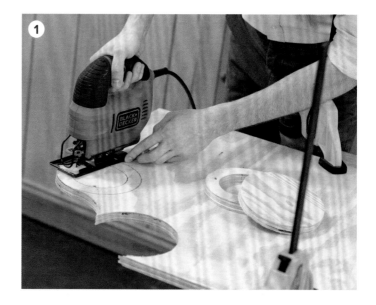

STEP 2: Clamp the solid disk to a work surface with a sacrificial piece underneath. Center a 1" spade bit on the center mark and drill a hole all the way through the disk. Use a jigsaw to cut a ½" wide slot in one of the rings, from the outside edge to the inside edge.

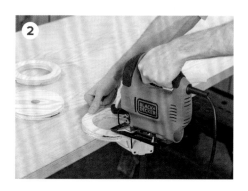

STEP 3: Sand all the cut edges smooth. Prime and paint the wood disks gloss white. Do the same with the two pine posts.

STEP 4: Position and mark the two posts directly opposite each other on the bottom disk. Drill pilot holes and screw through the underside of the disk into the posts. Position the un-notched ring centered on the post to match the position of the bottom disk. Drill pilot holes and screw the ring to the posts.

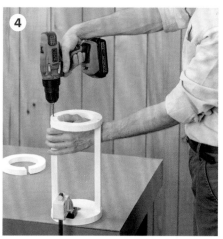

STEP 5: Secure the socket in the base disk center hole (the socket used here has wings that hold it in place; if yours doesn't, you can secure it with a dab of silicone glue). Screw a plastic cable clamp on the underside of the base disk about ¼" from the hole, and then another aligned with the first about 1" from the first. Holding the cord taut, screw the clamps over the cord.

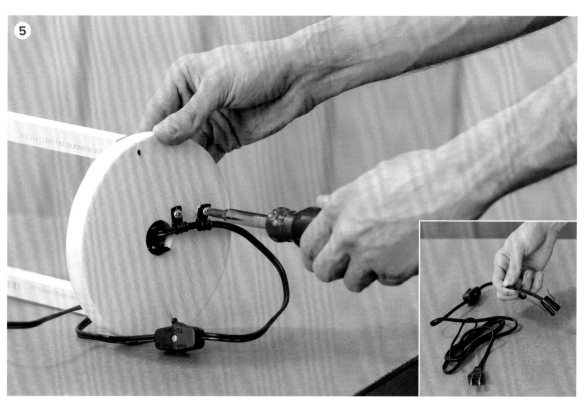

STEP 6: Turn the lamp frame upside down and clamp the notched ring to the base disk, aligned with it and with the cord running out through the slot cut in the ring. Drill countersunk pilot holes and screw the ring to the bottom disk with a series of 1¼" wood screws. Put a bulb in the lamp socket and plug it in to test that it is working.

STEP 7: Drill four holes spaced equally along one end of the aluminum sheet, ¼" in from the edge. Stand the lamp upright and hold the sheet edge to one of the posts. Drill pilot holes through the sheet holes, and screw the sheet to the post with ¾" wood screws.

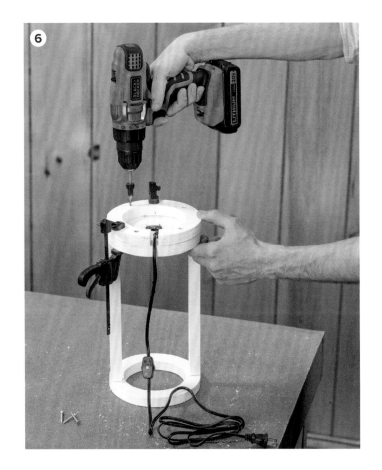

STEP 8: Roll the aluminum sheet tightly around the lamp frame. Clamp the sheet where it overlaps the screws holding the starting edge of the sheet. Mark the screw locations and the cut line.

STEP 9: Mark a notch for the electrical cord. Make the notch big enough so that the cord will not rub against a sharp metal edge. Unscrew the end of the sheet and remove the aluminum sheet from the frame.

STEP 10: Use tin snips to cut the sheet to length. Drill holes at the screw locations on the opposite end from the starting end. Cut the notch for the cord.

STEP 11: Position the aluminum sheet with the holes in the sheet aligned with the holes in the post and clamp the sheet in place around the frame. Screw through the holes in both ends (overlapping) and into the post. Drill pilot holes and screw a few additional screws around the top ring edge and bottom disk edge.

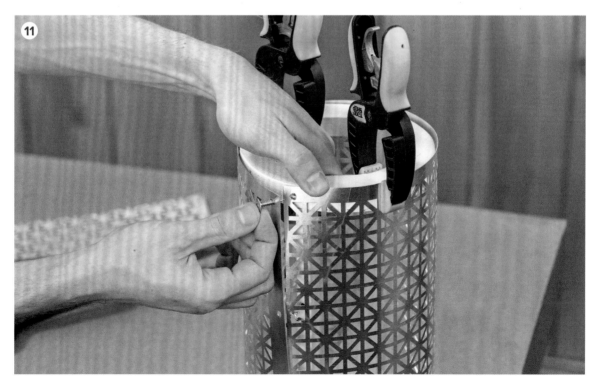

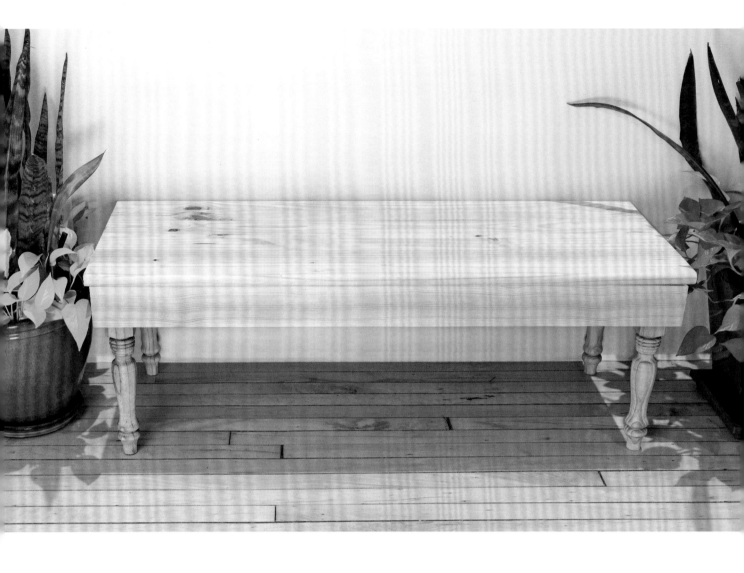

Bedroom or Entryway Bench

A bedroom bench is an often overlooked piece of furniture that should get more attention than it usually does. This is a traditional part of the bedroom furniture suite that adds an obvious design element, but, more importantly, provides day-to-day function that makes the bedroom much more convenient.

Think about it. How many times each day do you sit on the edge of your bed to put on socks and shoes, answer a phone call, or slip your pants on and off? Perching on the edge of a mattress is a sure way to decrease the lifespan of the mattress and is never very comfortable. A bench provides a place to sit and finish dressing, temporarily place a jacket or other clothing, or even keep a stack of books in the room. Once you add a bedroom bench to your sleeping chamber, you're likely to be surprised at how much you use it.

The bench in this project has been carefully designed to take up the smallest possible footprint while still being incredibly useful. It can be placed at the foot of the bed, where it won't get in the way of traffic flow in the room, and where it will be most accessible. However, you could just as easily place it along one wall in a larger bedroom, or anywhere that suits your preferred layout. You could also adapt it to other areas. It can, for instance, be wonderful seating for a vanity area, a place to rest while putting on makeup. The size and design make it ideal for duty in a large entryway, or as extra seating in a large living room. You could even increase the length of the legs and use this as a small side table.

Regardless, precision is key in this project. A wobbly, out-of-square bench is almost worse than no bench at all. Take your time when making the measurements and especially when you're checking alignment between different members, such as the legs and braces.

The design of the bench was developed for simple and sturdy construction. Traditionally, aprons on a bench are attached with mortise-and-tenon joints, but four concealed face-mount 2 × 4 joist hangers do the job here with no woodworking skills required. The seat is made of stair treads, available through home centers everywhere. The milled bullnose on these treads make for a comfortable edge on the seat. The stair treads are unfinished and could be painted or stained instead of finished clear. If you're willing to spend a little bit more money, you could even opt for stair treads in one of the many different woods and finishes (many stair treads come prefinished). Although the base here is natural, it could just as easily be painted or stained.

WHAT YOU NEED:

MATERIALS
- ▶ (2) 11¼ × 48" unfinished pine stair tread
- ▶ (4) 2¼ × 2¼ × 15¼" turned legs
- ▶ (2) 1 × 4 × 96" pine board
- ▶ (2) 2 × 4 × 96" pine board
- ▶ (4) 2 × 4" face-mount joist hangers
- ▶ 80-grit sandpaper

- ▶ 2" wood screws
- ▶ 1" wood screws
- ▶ Finishing nails
- ▶ Wood putty
- ▶ Wood conditioner
- ▶ Paste wax

TOOLS
- ▶ Measuring tape
- ▶ Carpenter's pencil
- ▶ Speed square
- ▶ Nailset
- ▶ Miter saw or adjustable table saw
- ▶ Circular saw
- ▶ Power drill and bits
- ▶ Palm sander (optional)
- ▶ Paintbrush

- ▶ Putty knife
- ▶ Carpenter's level
- ▶ Hammer
- ▶ Metal straightedge
- ▶ Bar clamps
- ▶ Cheesecloth applicator
- ▶ Eye and ear protection
- ▶ Work gloves

BEDROOM BENCH CUT LIST

KEY	QTY	PART NAME	DIMENSION	MATERIAL
A	4	Legs	2¼ × 2¼ × 1¼"	Turned pine
B	2	Seatboard	1 9½ × 48"	Pine stair tread
C	3	Frame blocking	1½ × 3½ × 12⅝"	Pine
D	2	Frame Side	1½ × 3½ × 40½"	Pine
E	2	Apron end	¾ × 3½ × 18"	Pine
F	2	Apron side	¾ × 3½ × 47"	Pine

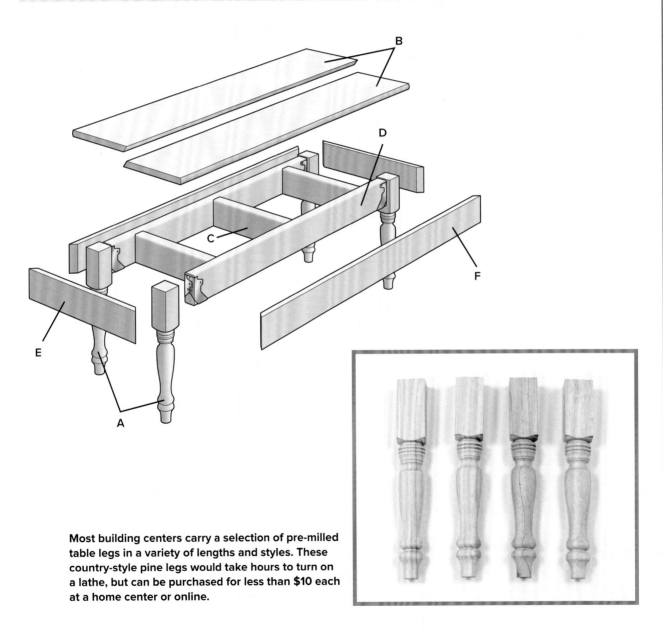

Most building centers carry a selection of pre-milled table legs in a variety of lengths and styles. These country-style pine legs would take hours to turn on a lathe, but can be purchased for less than $10 each at a home center or online.

How to Build a Bedroom or Entryway Bench

STEP 1: Use a joist hanger and 2 × 4 end scrap to measure and mark the frame position on one face of all the legs. The hangers should be centered side to side on the faces, and the 2 × 4 should be flush with the top of the leg.

STEP 2: After you've marked all the faces, screw the hangers to the legs with #14 self-tapping screws.

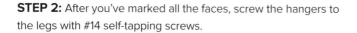

THE TOOL AISLE

Orbital Sander Shopping Guide

When it comes to hand sanders, the finest touch can be had with orbital sanders. However, there are actually two, fairly different types of orbital sander: the orbital finishing sander with a square pad and the random orbital sander with a round pad. In either case, they are sometimes called quarter pad sanders, because that's how much of a standard sandpaper sheet they use at a time.

- **Orbital finishing sander.** This sander is effective for easy smoothing tasks where not a lot of material needs to be removed—such as between paint coats and light sanding of a wood surface. Models with holding clips are less expensive, because it usually entails cutting down a standard sandpaper sheet to clip on the pad. If you prefer the convenience of stick-on pads and don't mind paying a premium for the sandpaper, look for a model with a stick pad. The other key factor is comfort. The sander should feel very good in your hand, or you'll quickly fatigue when sanding. The length of warranty is a good indicator of value with this type of sander, and a quality model is bound to last far longer than the cheapest you'll find.

- **Random orbital sander.** Unlike standard orbital sanders on which the pad spins like a wheel, the random orbital sander sands with a random movement that doesn't leave circular sanding marks. Although it's handheld like the smaller orbital finishing sander, it is more powerful and capable of knocking down significant putty buildup and rough work pieces. The best random orbital sanders feature a "hook-and-loop" pad attachment that holds the pad firm during sanding. You'll also want to find one with variable speeds rather than a simple off and on setting, because the speeds offer a great deal more control. As with an orbital finishing sander, grip is hugely important. Look for abundant padding under your palm and plenty of purchase area for your fingers. If you do a lot of sanding, consider paying more for a unit with a vacuum attachment to remove dust quickly and efficiently.

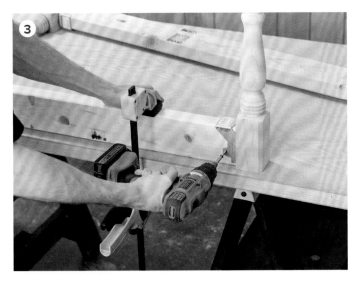

STEP 3: Cut the 2 × 4 frame sides to length and sand the ends smooth. Insert the ends into the joist hanger hardware attached to the leg tops. Fasten with #14 1¼" screws. Work on a flat, level work table with the bench upside down to ensure the top will be perfectly flat.

STEP 4: Sit the leg assemblies upside down on a flat, level work surface, parallel and about 16½" apart (measured outside to outside). Position one frame block between the leg assemblies, centered along their length. Place the other two frame blocks 4" in from either end. Check that the blocks are square to the frame sides, and that the frame is square, then screw the frame sides to the blocking ends with 3" screws.

STEP 5: Cut the aprons to length and sand the ends. Position the apron ends across the ends of the legs, flush to the sides and tops of the legs. Drill pilot holes through the aprons into the legs, and tack the legs in place with 4d finish nails. Repeat with the side aprons, overlapping the ends of the sides to form butt joints with the apron ends.

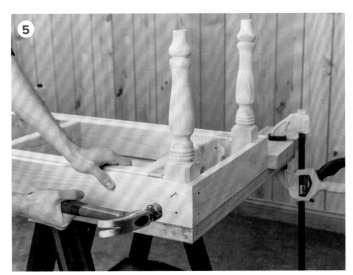

STEP 6: Use a nail set to set all the finish nails in the aprons. Cover all the heads with wood putty (inset). Let dry and sand smooth.

STEP 7: Center the bench seat boards on the top of the frame, and clamp in place. Drill pilot holes and fasten the seat boards in place with 4d finish nails. Use a nailset to sink the nails. Putty over the nail heads and sand smooth.

STEP 8: Finish the bench with a coat of wood conditioner and your choice of stain, clear poly, or paint. (The bench here was finished with Swedish Maple stain for a "country" look.) Pine is a very porous wood, so it is always a good idea to give the wood a coat of wood conditioner before applying stain. It will provide a more even finish with less blotchiness.

STEP 9: Protect the finish and bench with a coat of paste wax, buffed on with a cheesecloth applicator. Buffing the wax is a very critical step in finishing. The more you buff, the glossier and harder the finish becomes.

Living Wall

If you're looking for an entirely novel way to introduce a living decorative centerpiece—look no further. The stunning structure in this project frames a wealth of plants of your choosing. Go with annual flowers for a display bursting with colors, create an incredibly varied vertical herb garden for a sunny kitchen wall, or just enjoy a cascade of foliage year round with a combination of mounding and trailing perennials.

The wonderful thing about this unique creation is that it works equally well inside or out. All you really need is an abundance of light, because you control the growing medium and type of plants. You can even grow this wall in low-light situations by installing the optional gro-light fixture (page 85).

The construction is a bit unusual, but not technically challenging. The project has been designed to support what can add up to considerable weight—when you combine lumber, soil, plants, and water. The structure is basically a U-shaped outer cabinet, kept secure with spreaders, and with a 2 × 4 frame in the center that supports a prefab fabric "planting pocket" hanging wall. (These are widely available in garden centers and online.) When filled, the fabric allows water and air to pass through, but securely holds soil and plant roots. If leakage is a concern, use the catcher described in the instructions.

WHAT YOU NEED:

MATERIALS

- 2" drywall screws
- 2½" deck screws
- Wood glue
- 39 × 39" felt wall planter
- 80-grit sandpaper
- Wood putty
- Black paint
- Paint, stain, or finish

TOOLS

- Circular saw
- Power drill and bits
- Putty knife
- Paintbrush
- Eye and ear protection
- Work gloves

LIVING WALL CUT LIST

KEY	QTY	PART NAME	DIMENSION	MATERIAL
A	2	Cabinet sides	1 × 7¼ × 80"	Select Pine
B	1	Cabinet top	1 × 7¼ × 39"	Select Pine
C	1	Bottom Spreader	1 × 5¼ × 19"	Pine
D	1	Top Spreader	1 × 3½ × 39"	Pine
E	2	Frame Horizontal	1½ × 3½ × 39"	SPF
F	2	Frame Vertical	1½ × 3½ × 32"	SPF

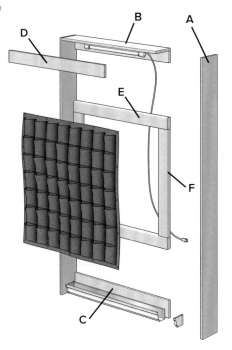

How to Build a Living Wall

STEP 1: Glue and screw the top between the sides with wood glue and 2½" drywall screws driven through pilot holes.

STEP 2: Working on a flat, level work surface, lay a 1 × 4 top spreader between the two sides, and butted to the top. Drill pilot holes and screw the sides to the spreader. Install a 1 × 6 bottom spreader at the opposite end in the same way, between the two sides and flush with the ends of the sides. Flip the structure and add top and bottom spreaders to the opposite side of the structure.

STEP 3: Lay the 2 × 4s for the interior frame on a flat, level work surface. The shorter verticals should run inside the longer horizontals. Toenail the frame together at the corners, ensuring it is square.

STEP 4: Insert the frame into the cabinet. The top should be 18" down from the top of the cabinet. Position the frame square to the cabinet. (The back of the frame top should be flush with the back of the cabinet.) Tilt the bottom of the frame up 2", using shims. This will ensure light reaches the plants in the lower pockets. Secure the frame with 2½" deck screws driven through the sides and into the ends and edges of the frame.

STEP 5: Putty over nail and screw heads, let dry, and sand smooth. Paint the exterior of the carcass whatever color you desire, then paint the interior and frame black (a dark color won't show through the plantings as much).

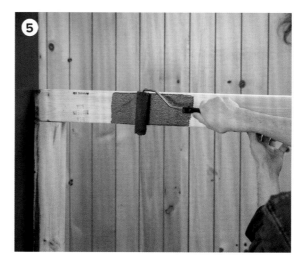

STEP 6: Secure the felt wall planter to the frame. The version shown here has brass grommets, allowing the planter to be hung with zip ties. However, to ensure proper support for watersoaked plants and soil, the planter was screwed to the frame with 1¼" pole barn screws.

OPTIONAL: Install a grow light in the top of the cabinet if you plan on locating the living wall indoors, or in any low-light area. Center the fixture on the underside of the cabinet top, as far toward the front of the cabinet as possible, and screw it to the cabinet with ½" wood screws. NOTE: To make the light maintenance-free, fasten an in-line timer on the exterior of the cabinet, and plug the light's power cord into the timer.

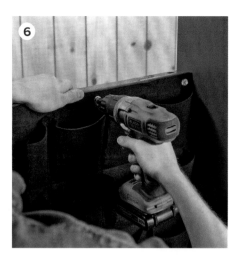

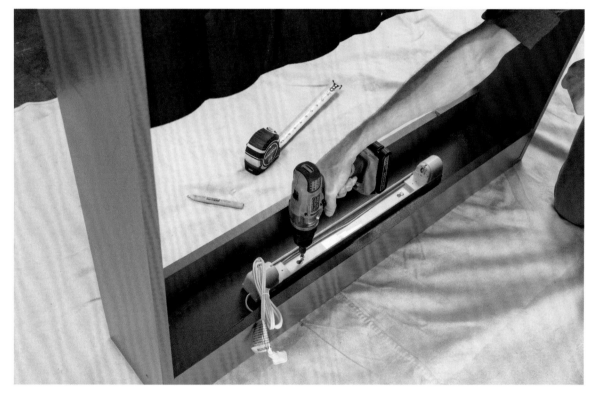

QUICK TIP

Waterproof

When you water the plants in this living wall, there is a chance that excess water will leak out of the pockets. If you don't want them leaking on a surface below where the living wall is located, create a water catcher. Cut a section of 6" K-profile metal or vinyl gutter slightly shorter than the width of the cabinet. Glue gutter end caps on either end and sit the gutter under the felt planter (or attach it between the cabinet sides).

Plant Stand

If you've gone to the effort of nurturing an indoor plant with lovely foliage and an attractive growing habit, it seems a shame to hide it on a side table or off in a corner of a bookshelf. Great indoor plants need a stage to shine, and a table like the one in this project is just the pedestal on which to show off your botanical lovelies.

The stand has been designed with its function in mind; the look is subdued and sophisticated, not so showy as to steal attention away from your favorite plant, but not so dull as to fade into the background. It helps that the construction is sturdy—the stand can tolerate the burden of even a heavy plant in a true terra cotta pot with moist soil. The inclusion of ceramic tile surfaces on the shelves ensures that a little leakage is not going to be a problem and that cleanup will be a breeze.

You'll also find that the tiny footprint of the stand allows you to put it just about anywhere, from the corner of a solarium or sunny living room, to fitting right by a front door, enjoying the sun streaming through entryway sidelites. No matter what, though, position the stand for the benefit and light exposure needs of the plant on top.

WHAT YOU NEED

MATERIALS

- ▶ (1) 1 × 8 × 48" (pine or poplar) board
- ▶ (2) 1 × 3 × 120" (pine or poplar) board
- ▶ (1) ½ × 1 × 96" (pine or poplar) stop molding
- ▶ (1) 8 × 4' × ½" plywood
- ▶ (1) 12" square ceramic tile
- ▶ (1) 7½" square or mosaic tile
- ▶ 150-grit sandpaper
- ▶ Wood glue
- ▶ 3d and 4d finish nails
- ▶ 1", 1¼" and 1½" deck screws
- ▶ Wood putty

TOOLS

- ▶ Power drill and bits
- ▶ Circular saw
- ▶ Palm sander
- ▶ V-notch adhesive trowel
- ▶ Grout float
- ▶ Nailset
- ▶ Putty knife
- ▶ Masking tape
- ▶ Eye and ear protection
- ▶ Work gloves

PLANT STAND CUT LIST

KEY	QTY	PART NAME	DIMENSION	MATERIAL
A	4	Box side	¾ × 7¼" × 8"	Pine
B	8	Leg	¾ × 2½ × 29½"	Pine
C	1	Top tile base	1½ × 12¼ × 12¼"	Plywood
D	1	Box top	¾ × 7¼ × 7¼"	Pine
E	1	Shelf	½ × 7¾ × 7¾"	Plywood
F	4	Top frame	½ × 1 × 13¼"	Pine Molding
G	4	Shelf frame	½ × 1 × 8¾"	Pine Molding

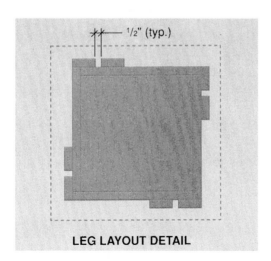

LEG LAYOUT DETAIL

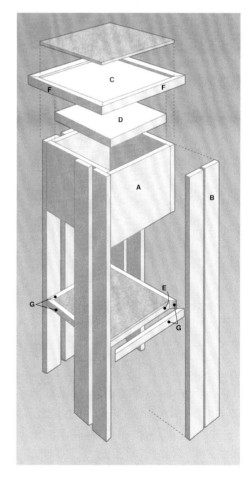

How to Build a Plant Stand

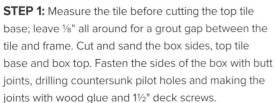

STEP 1: Measure the tile before cutting the top tile base; leave ⅛" all around for a grout gap between the tile and frame. Cut and sand the box sides, top tile base and box top. Fasten the sides of the box with butt joints, drilling countersunk pilot holes and making the joints with wood glue and 1½" deck screws.

STEP 2: Center the box top on the bottom face of the top tile base. Drive 1" deck screws through the top tile base and into the box top.

STEP 3: Position the top tile base and box top onto the box. Drill countersunk pilot holes through the box sides and into the top. Fasten the box top with 1½" deck screws.

STEP 4: Drill countersunk pilot holes through the legs and into the box sides. Ensure that each outside leg is flush with the box edge before attaching the legs with wood glue and 1¼" decks screws. Maintain a ¼" gap between the legs in each pair.

STEP 5: Miter the shelf frame board ends. Spread tile adhesive on the shelf, using a V-notch trowel. Press the tile into place, centered on the shelf. Let the adhesive cure fully before proceeding.

STEP 6: Drill pilot holes and nail the shelf frame pieces in place around the shelf with 3d finish nails. The top of the shelf frame should be level with the top of the tile.

STEP 7: Drill pilot holes and nail the legs to the lower shelf with 4d finish nails. (The bottom of the shelf should be 10" from the bottom of the stand.)

STEP 8: Miter each end of the top frame pieces. Attach the top tile to the top tile base as you did with the lower tile and base.

STEP 9: Drill pilot holes and nail the top frame in place against the top base, using 4d finish nails and keeping the top edges of the frame flush with the top of the tile. Be careful to drive the nails into the base, rather than the tile.

STEP 10: Set all the nails with a nailset. Cover nail and screw heads with wood putty, let dry, and sand smooth. Finish sand all surfaces with 150-grit sandpaper. Prime and paint the stand as desired (or finish natural with two coats of clear polyurethane if desired).

STEP 11: Once the finish is dry, mask off the frame pieces and fill the gaps between the tiles and the frames with tinted grout. Use a small grout float to pack the grout into the gaps and smooth the joints with a damp sponge.

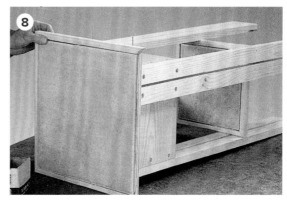

Five-Gallon Planter

Impressive planters can be showcases in a backyard setting. Sizeable, substantial, and unusual planters are often the perfect addition to deck, patio, or backyard. It can even be a surprising visual in the garden proper, a perfect place for a lovely specimen plant amid permanent plantings or shrub stands. Large, sturdy planters allow you to control the sun exposure, soil, and water culture of the plant, keeping it super healthy. The planter also lets you put the plant where you'll get the most visual bang for the buck.

The one downside? Cost. Large ceramic planters can run more than $100 and that's not counting the eye-catching plants they call for.

But there's a much better way to get your ideal large planter than running out to the local nursery or home center. You can make a visually and physically sturdy planter with just a few basic supplies from different aisles in the home center.

A planter like the one in this project can be adapted to many different plants and applications. You can modify the look in many different ways, and making multiples requires just a bit more work than making one. The best part is that you don't need the high-end skills that making a large ceramic planter would require—and the result will look every bit as cool.

This planter is heavy enough that rambunctious pets, children playing tag, or the occasional fierce summer thunderstorm won't tip it over. The planter is a clever use of the common 5-gallon plastic bucket, which you can buy from any home center or hardware store or even find free at many different supermarkets and other retailers (just clean it out before use). With a little time and a modest amount of elbow grease, you'll have stunning backyard addition that will be the envy of the neighbors.

WHAT YOU NEED:

MATERIALS

- 5-gallon plastic bucket
- 80-grit sandpaper
- Heavy-duty duct tape
- ½" wood dowel
- 8"-dia. tube form
- Nonstick cooking spray
- Quick-setting concrete mix
- Latex concrete fortifier
- Fiber mesh reinforcement

TOOLS

- Marker
- Straightedge
- Square
- Reciprocating saw
- Hot glue gun and glue
- Concrete mixing supplies
- Trowel
- Utility knife
- Diamond polishing pad
- Eye and ear protection
- Work gloves

Make a Five-Gallon Planter

STEP 1: Turn the five-gallon bucket upside down and use a marker and a carpenter's square to draw a line across the center of the bottom. Use the square to extend the line on each side, up the sides of the bucket.

STEP 2: Cut the bucket in half with a reciprocating saw fit with a fine-tooth blade. Cut down both sides first, then across the bottom. Smooth the cut edges with sandpaper.

STEP 3: Reassemble the two halves of the bucket with duct tape. Run the tape along the cut lines, then wrap two or more horizontal bands of tape around the circumference of the bucket.

STEP 4: Hot-glue a 3"-long, ½" dowel or pipe to the bottom center of the bucket to create a drainage hole for the planter. Coat the inside of the bucket, the dowel, and the outside of the cardboard tube form with nonstick cooking spray or concrete release treatment.

STEP 5: Mix quick-setting concrete with a latex fortifier; make the concrete stiff rather than wet and sloppy. Add 2" of the mix to the bottom of the bucket and tap the bucket on a hard work surface to settle the concrete. Optionally, add fiber reinforcement (or use a concrete mix containing fiber mesh) for extra durability.

STEP 6: Set the cardboard tube form onto the top of the concrete layer, centering it inside the bucket. Fill around the tube with concrete, settling it periodically by striking the side of the bucket. Keep the tube centered in the bucket as you work. Smooth the concrete flush with the top of the bucket and let the casting cure for a day or more.

STEP 7: Free the planter by removing the tape around the bucket and pulling off the bucket halves. Slide out the tube form. (If the form is stuck, cut it from the inside with a utility knife and roll it inward to remove it.) Clean up the outside and top edge of the planter with a diamond pad or file, as desired.

Message Center

Chances are that if you're like most homeowners, your refrigerator is covered with a magnetic to-do pad, a grocery list, and a few other important pieces of paper in among the collage of family pictures or your collection of refrigerator magnets from everywhere you've traveled. Maybe you've even stuck up important papers that you don't want to forget to mail. Similarly, the wall over your guest bedroom work desk might be mottled with handwritten sticky notes recording upcoming events and pressing issues that require your attention. Maybe you even have a chalkboard somewhere in the house, listing chores or other family notices.

All of that should not be confused with true organization. There's a much better way to keep you and your family running smoothly through your lives. A centralized message center—one that is as handsome as it is useful—is the answer.

The stunning center outlined in the steps that follow is brilliant in its combination of simplicity and usefulness. There are surfaces for writing and for sticking up important papers and handy hidden storage, all in a visually pleasing package with a bit of flair that ensures you'll be proud to mount this near the overused back door or right along a main wall in the kitchen.

Even better, this project doesn't require advanced workworking or DIY skills. You just need to be careful with the measurements and pay attention to the details, and the message center will look like something you ordered out of a furniture catalog. Just don't be surprised when friends hound you to know where you got it.

WHAT YOU NEED

MATERIALS

- ► (1) ⁴⁄₄ × 8" × 10' deck board
- ► (1) ⁴⁄₄ × 6" × 8' deck board
- ► (1) 1 × 4 × 4' pine
- ► (1) ½ × 48 × 48" birch plywood

- ► 2 touch latches
- ► Panel adhesive
- ► 2" finish nails
- ► (4) 2" butt hinges

- ► (4) ½ × 12 × 12" cork tiles
- ► Wood glue
- ► 2" finish nails

TOOLS

- ► Miter saw or circular saw and miter guide
- ► Power drill and bits

- ► Bar clamps
- ► Hammer

- ► Eye and ear protection
- ► Work gloves

MESSAGE CENTER CUT LIST

KEY	QTY	PART NAME	DIMENSION	MATERIAL
A	2	Top/Bottom	⁴⁄₄ × 7¼ × 48"	Select Pine
B	1	Side	⁴⁄₄ × 7¼ × 26¼"	Select Pine
C	2	Divider	⁴⁄₄ × 5½ × 24¼"	Select Pine
D	1	Cork backer	½ × 24 × 24"	Birch plywood
E	1	Dry erase backer	½ × 12 × 24"	Birch plywood
F	1	Cleat	½ × 3 × 24¼"	Birch plywood

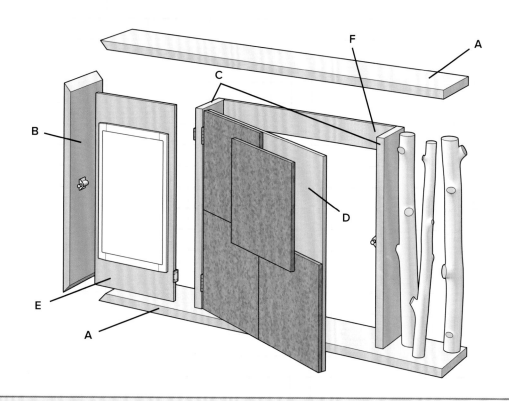

How to Build a Message Center

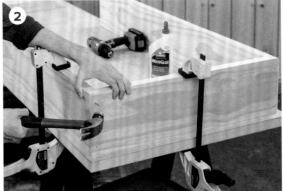

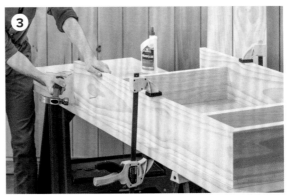

STEP 1: After cutting the top and bottom boards to the dimensions on the cutting list, make 45° bevel cuts at one end of each using a power miter saw (or a circular saw and cutting guide). Cut mating bevels at each end of the side board to fit with the beveled ends of the top and bottom.

STEP 2: Cut the dividers from nominal 6" wide ¾ stock (or use leftover 8" stock and trim off 2" from the back edge).

STEP 3: Fasten the bevel joints between the side and the top and bottom boards using wood glue, 2" finish nails, and clamps.

STEP 4: Measure and mark the divider positions to create a 12¼"-wide dry-erase bay, and a 24¼"-wide cork-board bay. Use wood glue and 2" finish nails to fasten the two dividers between the top and bottom boards, flush with the back edges.

STEP 5: Cut the mounting panels for the cork board and dry erase board, using a circular saw and straightedge cutting guide. Sand the edges smooth.

STEP 6: Cut the hanger cleat from plywood or scrap and fasten it to the top board in the cork bay, between the dividers, using glue and finish nails. The cleat should be flush to the back of the board.

STEP 7: Use panel adhesive to attach the dry erase board to the backer, centered on the backer. Use the sticky tabs supplied with the cork panels (shown) or use panel adhesive to fasten the cork tiles to the corkboard backer.

STEP 8: Hang the dry erase board and the corkboard in their bays, screwing 2" butt hinges attached to opposite sides of the divider that separates the two bays.

STEP 9: Install touch latches inside the corkboard cabinet opening and the dry erase board opening. OPTIONAL: Cut and install a narrow shelf inside the corkboard bay. Finish or paint the message center as desired.

STEP 10: Cut three or four decorative 1" dia. branches to fit vertically in the open area at the right of the message center. Position them in the opening in a pleasing composition. Toenail them in place with finish nails, or drill screw holes from underneath and screw the branches in place.

STEP 11: Hang the message center by driving a pair of screws through the cleat and into wall studs.

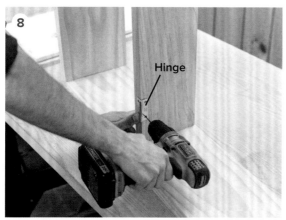

Hinge

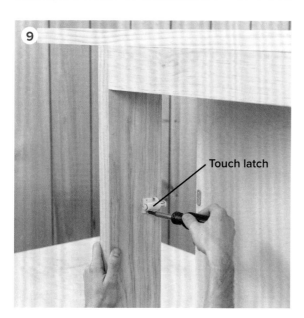

Touch latch

Birdhouse

Imagine stepping out into your backyard on a sunny morning, cup of coffee in your hand, and watching as beautiful songbirds fill the air with music and color. It's a wonderful way to start the day, but one that doesn't happen by accident.

Birds, like humans, flock to places that attract them. Just as humans tend to land in pretty towns or vibrant bustling cities that offer services, safety, and nice places to live, birds seek sanctuaries where they can rest protected from predators and where they can find sustenance without too much work.

The house in this project is specifically designed to be constructed with minimal expense, expertise, and effort. You should be able to use lumber odds and ends left over from other projects, with just a few crucial hardware and supplies that can easily be found in any well-stocked hardware store. With that in mind, don't hesitate to alter the dimensions to suit the pieces you have on hand. There are, however, certain features that should not be changed. For instance, there is a key easy-access element on the birdhouse—a removable bottom on the birdhouse—that is essential to the success of this backyard addition. The removable bottom allows you to clean out the unit when birds are not using it, which is crucial to keeping birds healthy and free from parasites and insects.

The outside appearance is less crucial, but certainly worth consideration. The instructions for the house include painting it a simple green, which will be pleasing for any birds. You can change the color scheme as you see fit, but keep in mind that birds have keen eyesight and prefer something that looks natural to them. It's a good idea to stay away from a pure white birdhouse, because many species consider white a sign of alarm and danger. You'll notice that no perches have been added. Perches can be used by predator birds to dominate the feeder and attack nesting birds.

Adding a birdhouse to your yard is also a responsibility. You should keep the area clear of debris and overgrowth that could hide predators. The reward for paying a little attention and thought to your backyard birdhouse and bird feeder will be a nearly nonstop show of colorful flying creatures and pleasing birdsong.

WHAT YOU NEED:

MATERIALS

- 80-grit sandpaper
- 4" PVC pipe
- (2) 4" PVC slip caps
- PVC primer and cement
- ¼" dowel
- 1¼" flathead wood screws
- ¾" round head screws
- Plastic primer and paint, and exterior gloss paint
- Painter's tape
- #14 zinc- or nickel-plated chain (or substitute paracord or similar)
- #8 screw hook

TOOLS

- Table saw or miter saw
- Bar clamps
- Carpenter's compass
- Metal straightedge
- Center punch or awl
- Palm sander (optional)
- Power drill and bits
- 1¼" hole saw
- Eye and ear protection
- Work gloves

Creating a Birdhouse

Like all of us, birds seek a comfortable place to rest their weary (hollow) bones. But birds have different requirements than humans when it comes to comfortable lodgings. Comfort, for a feathered home resident, means being safe amid familiar and secure surroundings. That means that creating the most attractive home for potential lodgers is a matter both of where you put the house and how appealing your yard is from a bird's perspective.

To start with, the birdhouse should be at roughly the correct height for the species you're hoping to attract (see box "Size Matters" on page 103). But you should also follow the guidelines below to ensure the birdhouse is exactly where the birds would most like to stay. Any feeder you add should be kept even higher, as far away from the birdhouse as reasonable, and away from any location where squirrels or raccoons could drop onto the feeder (keeping in mind that you'll still need to get to the feeder to refill the birdseed).

- **Line of sight.** Clear line of sight is important for birds and human minders. Enjoying the birds that come into your yard means being able to see them, so the birdhouse should be placed where it can be directly viewed from windows in the house, or a common area such as a backyard deck. Not only does this ensure that you enjoy the activities of your many feathered friends, it allows you to detect any potential dangers, such as feral cats, before they cause problems. But line of sight also applies to what the birds can see. They should be able to view in all directions before entering the house, so that they can make sure the coast is clear whenever they come home.

- **Keep it clear.** Although birds tend to like landscaping that mimics what they would find in the wild, they choose a home based on safety. The safest birdhouse is farther than a cat's jump from a nearby branch or surface. It should be away from fences or other features that might conceal a predator.

- **Off the beaten path.** Birds like to nest in relative quiet, away from commotion. Place a birdhouse away from common areas where people and pets frequently tread. Even if humans and animals aren't actually close to the birdhouse, the constant motion will cause birds to stay away.

How to Build a Birdhouse

STEP 1: Screw a 1 × 4 sacrificial wood piece to the miter saw fence. Clamp the PVC pipe to the fence and cut it 8" long, slowly and carefully. Sand the pipe and two caps all over—including sanding down any raised lettering—until they are an even, matte white and a uniform color.

- **Watch the windows.** Birdhouses should be kept as far from windows as possible to prevent birds flying into the windows and injuring themselves. This may not be a problem for house windows, because most people instinctively know to place a birdhouse at a remove from the house where human activity is common. But the same holds true for outbuilding windows, such as those in a utility shed.

- **Landscape with safe, native plants.** The ideal birding landscape includes a variety of plants that birds know, trust, and see as potential food and shelter. Part of that landscaping involves avoiding any plants that could be toxic to birds. For example, caster bean, Lily of the Valley, and foxglove are all potentially poisonous to birds in the garden. Keep in mind that if you have fruits such as a cherry tree, the birds are going to take their share. Most bird lovers accept that as a fair bargain.

- **Limit the lawn.** An expanse of grass is of little use or attraction to a songbird. If you really want to create an inviting environment for winged visitors, replace all or part of a large lawn with flowering shrubs or trees.

- **Account for weather.** If your area is subject to severe storms and high winds, create a wind break to prevent the birdhouse from being blown off its support.

STEP 2: Use a carpenter's compass or a nail, string, and pencil, to measure and mark two circles on the plywood, one 5" in diameter and one 7" in diameter. Use a jigsaw to cut out the discs. Use a jigsaw or 3" hole saw to cut out a 3" disc from the center of the 7" disc. Cut the dowel 6" long.

STEP 3: Clamp the PVC pipe in a vise with padded jaws, or to a work surface using bar clamps. Use a metal rule as a straightedge, laid end to end, and mark the bird access hole 5" in from one end. Use a center punch or awl to mark a starting point and drill the hole with a 1¼" hole saw. Sand the edges of the hole smooth.

STEP 4: Turn one of the slip caps upside down on the work surface and lay a straightedge directly across the center of the cap. Mark the lip on both sides, for holes directly across from one another. Run the marks down onto the sides of the cap (the holes should be drilled ¾" down from the edge of the lip). Secure the cap in a vise with padded jaws, and make a drill-bit starting point at one of the key marks, using an awl or center punch. Drill a ¼" dowel hole at the mark. Remove any burrs around the hole with sandpaper or a utility knife.

STEP 5: Slide the dowel through the hole and check where the dowel contacts the lip on the opposite side. Ensure that the contact point matches the key marks. Remove the dowel and drill the opposite hole as you did the first. Stand the pipe on a work surface with the bottom up (the end on which the drilled slip cap will be placed). Slip the drilled cap onto the pipe, and use the holes on each side as guides to drill matching holes in the base of the pipe.

STEP 6: Use a compass to draw a 3" circle on the 5" disc. Lay the 3" disc on the circle and flip the two discs. Drill four pilot holes at points of the compass, and screw the 5" disc to the 3" disc with 1¼" flathead wood screws, being careful to keep the 3" disc centered.

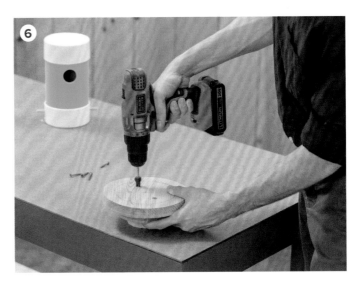

STEP 7: Center the 7" disc on top of the 5" disc as you did in the previous step. Drill two pilot holes on either side and screw the 7" disc to the 5" disc with 1¼" flathead wood screws. Set the undrilled slip cap top down, centered on the 7" disc. Screw the cap to the 7" disc with two ¾" round head screws spaced evenly around the inside of the cap.

STEP 8: Cement the top of the pipe into the undrilled slip cap with PVC primer and cement (follow the instructions on the tin).

STEP 9: Lightly sand the wood, PVC pieces, and dowel. Lay a very fine bead of exterior white paintable caulk along the joints between the wood discs. Tape off the wood pieces and prime and paint the plastic sections with gloss white plastic paint. Let it dry, then tape off the plastic pieces, and prime and paint the wood gloss white, using quality exterior paint. Slip the drilled cap onto the end of the pipe and align the holes. Tap the dowel through the holes. (If the holes are too large and the dowel is loose, dab a small amount of silicone adhesive around the holes.)

STEP 10: Drill a pilot hole and install a screw hook into the top of the birdhouse. Hang it from a sturdy tree branch with a length of #14 nickel-plated chain, nylon string, or similar.

QUICK TIP

Size Matters

The entrance hole in this project's birdhouse is 1¼" in diameter, but different species prefer different size holes. It's a matter of being able to fit through, while preventing predators from getting in.

Bird	Hole Size	Placement Height from Ground
Eastern Bluebird	1½"	8' high, in open area
Tree Swallow	1"	6–8' high, in open area
Purple Martin	2⅛"	20' high
Tufted Titmouse	1¼"	8–10' high
Chickadee	1⅛"	6–8' high
Nuthatch	1¼"	20–25' high
Wren	1"	8–10' high

Built-Ins from Stock Cabinetry

Walk into any large home center and you'll have no difficulty finding a simply awe-inspiring selection of cabinets and molding options. Modern cabinetry comes in an incredible diversity of attractive styles and durable materials. Stock models range from the plain to ornate, and regardless of which you choose, the prices have never been more attractive.

The projects in this section make good—if sometimes unconventional—use of stock cabinetry to create alluring work spaces and more. The key here is that it's easy to work with cabinetry because the dimensions are a known quantity. That means it's usually not very difficult to make adjustments as needed to suit the space available.

However, there's no getting around the fact that these projects are larger and more involved than most of those in the previous section. Just the same, the focus remains on basic skills, and ease of building. After all, that's the whole point of using readymade materials like prebuilt cabinets. So although the final version of any project in this section will be impressive and even room-changing, none will require fine woodworking experience, specialized tools, or techniques you've never heard of. The biggest challenge you'll face with these projects is choosing the one (or ones) that is just right for you house and how you want to work and live in it.

IN THIS SECTION:

Bed Surround

Do you still have your boring old headboard that came with your bed back when you bought it? If so, you're wasting a lot of dynamic real estate that could be put to far better use. All that area around where you lay your head at night is just begging to be exploited.

A full surround is the perfect treatment for adding massive amounts of accessible bedroom storage and injecting a lot of wow power into the look of your bedroom. This particular project includes nightstands on either side that are the very definition of "handy."

Because nobody will be walking under the cabinets, the overall measurements for placement are very forgiving and adjustable. It's wise to lay out the design on paper if you anticipate that you might want to change the dimensions supplied here. Standard queen-size mattresses are all the same dimensions, and your bed frame may add both width and height to the overall picture.

You can vary the look of your own surround with the cabinets you choose, and especially with the countertop materials you opt for in building the nightstands on either side of the bed. It's a place where you can splurge on upscale materials without breaking the bank. You can also add integral lighting fixtures with just a bit more work. However, the surround is also ideal for placement of screw-on corded fixtures that don't require dealing with wiring.

WHAT YOU NEED:

MATERIALS

- (4) 12 × 30" Wall cabinets
- (2) 15 × 30" Wall cabinet
- (2) 18 × 34½" Base cabinet

- (2) 1½ × 19 × 25" Countertop
- Spackle
- Sanding block

- Touch-up paint

TOOLS

- Measuring tape
- Stud finder
- Carpenter's pencil
- Power drill and bits

- Pull saw or coping saw
- Pry bar
- 4' level
- Circular saw

- Putty knife
- Eye and ear protection
- Work gloves

BED SURROUND CUT LIST

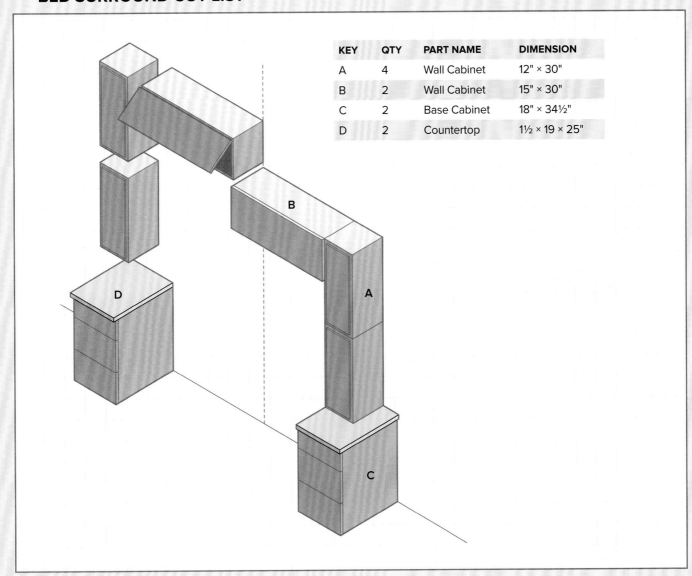

KEY	QTY	PART NAME	DIMENSION
A	4	Wall Cabinet	12" × 30"
B	2	Wall Cabinet	15" × 30"
C	2	Base Cabinet	18" × 34½"
D	2	Countertop	1½ × 19 × 25"

How to Build a Bed Surround

STEP 1: Mark the left and right edges of the project area based on your bed size (add about 1" on either side to the width of the bed), and then find the center between these two points. Be exact. Use a 4' level to mark a plumb line up from the center point on the wall. This is the control point from which you map out the rest of the layout.

STEP 2: Measure 30⅛" left and right of the center point to mark the outside edges of the horizontal uppers. (Drive a 6-penny nail right on the centerline to hold your tape.) Use a stud finder to locate and mark stud locations in the installation area.

STEP 3: Install a temporary ledger at the location of the bottom of the horizontal cabinets (81" above the floor in this case). Carefully install the horizontal upper cabinets by resting them in position on the ledger and driving screws through the cabinet backs and into wall studs.

STEP 4: Cut and install filler strips along the edge of any cabinet if there is a gap between it and its neighbor.

STEP 5: Use a 4' level to draw plumb lines down from the outside edges of the upper cabinets. Measure the base cabinets' width, and mark and cut out the baseboard from the plumb lines in, to accommodate the cabinet's width. Cut the baseboard with a coping or pull saw, and a pry bar as necessary. Be careful not to damage the drywall.

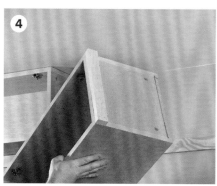

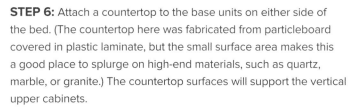

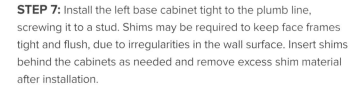

STEP 6: Attach a countertop to the base units on either side of the bed. (The countertop here was fabricated from particleboard covered in plastic laminate, but the small surface area makes this a good place to splurge on high-end materials, such as quartz, marble, or granite.) The countertop surfaces will support the vertical upper cabinets.

STEP 7: Install the left base cabinet tight to the plumb line, screwing it to a stud. Shims may be required to keep face frames tight and flush, due to irregularities in the wall surface. Insert shims behind the cabinets as needed and remove excess shim material after installation.

STEP 8: Mount the first vertical upper cabinet tight to the plumb line, on top of the left base cabinet, fastening it into a stud. Be careful of the countertop during installation. Mount the second vertical upper tight to the first. Make sure the face frames are flush and shim as necessary. Repeat for the right side vertical cabinets.

STEP 9: The horizontal uppers and vertical uppers should meet perfectly. If so, fasten the face frames with 2" wood screws.

STEP 10: If the cabinets are not flush, adjust the horizontal uppers to mate with the left and right vertical cabinet towers. Once flush in all directions, fasten the face frames and secure to the wall.

STEP 11: You can install (or have installed) any light fixtures and switches in the cabinet structure at this time. Remove the temporary ledger, patch the drywall, caulk, sand, and spot-touch the finishes and paint as necessary.

Closet Home Office

Carving out a dedicated home work space can be a real challenge. Even if you only use your home office part time, it's difficult to find an area where the debris of daily life won't creep in and make your work space much less organized. But there's a place to put a home office that might have slipped your attention this whole time. Right there in your own bedroom or a guest bedroom: a closet.

It doesn't even need to be a walk-in closet. Most standard closets have all the space you need—if configured correctly—to serve all your work needs and then some. It's just a matter of making the most of the available space, something this project was designed to help you do.

The beauty of installing a home office in a closet is that the space is self-contained and set apart from other spaces in the house. A closet conversion like the one in this project creates a discreet space where clutter is prevented through well-thought-out features that provide you with a place for everything you might need to store. There's also a lot of room to spread and be comfortable, whether you do most of your work on a computer, or work directly on paper.

This is a doable project for any homeowner with basic tools, the willingness to dive into a project and a free weekend to spend creating an ideal workspace. Once you've built it, you'll discover a great return on investment in the form of increased productive and a more comfortable place to earn a living.

QUICK TIP

Power

Provide electrical service to your office by branching off of an existing circuit. Here, boxes for a light fixture and a wall receptacle were added and wired to a room circuit. Patches for the drywall cut to route the wiring will be hidden by the panel and don't need a complete finish. Consult an electrician if this type of wiring is beyond your skill and comfort level.

WHAT YOU NEED:

MATERIALS
- Construction adhesive
- Finish nails (1¼", 2")
- 3½" wood screws
- 2¼" trimhead screws
- ⁵⁄₁₆" all-thread rod

- Hardwood-veneer MDF-core plywood (finish-grade on one side) (¼", ¾")
- Hanger bolts
- Coupling nuts
- Flat washers
- Hex nuts

- 1 × 1" and 1 × 2" maple
- ¾" particleboard with plastic laminate (on one side) for desktop
- Wood glue
- 1¼" coarse-thread drywall screws

TOOLS
- Caulk gun
- Circular saw and straightedge guide
- Level
- Drill with bits

- Hacksaw
- Wrench
- Sander
- Stud finder

- Clamps
- Eye and ear protection
- Work gloves

How to Build a Closet Home Office

STEP 1: Remove any baseboard and moldings in the closet. Make sure the wall is smooth and dust free. Locate and mark the wall studs (left photo); the panel seams should fall over stud centers. Optional: If you intend to panel the ceiling, locate the ceiling joists and map their locations on paper (right photo). (The joists support the suspended bookshelves, and it's difficult to locate joists once paneling is installed.)

STEP 2: Finish the good side of the paneling stock as desired. Cut the first panel to length. Cut from the back side with a circular saw to prevent splintering. Apply beads of construction adhesive to the back of the panel, and press the panel against the wall so the side edges are centered over studs.

STEP 3: Adjust the panel so it's perfectly plumb, then nail it to the wall studs with 1¼" finish nails. Use the nails sparingly; you need only enough to ensure the panel stays flat and the edges are securely and evenly adhered.

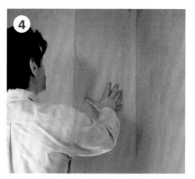

STEP 4: Cut and install the remaining panels. Use the straight factory edges for the butted seams. At the inside corners, place the second (perpendicular) panel with its factory edge butted against the first panel. If the seams are tight, you don't need to hide them with molding.

STEP 5: Plan the bookshelf spacing as desired, then draw level lines onto the walls to represent the bottom edge of each shelf. Cut and install 1 × 1 shelf cleats so their top edges are flush with the level lines. Fasten the cleats with 2¼" screws driven into wall studs.

STEP 6: Cut the shelves from ¾" plywood. The top and middle shelves are L-shaped, 11" deep along the back wall, with an 18"-long, full-depth leg at one end. The bottom shelf matches the leg dimensions. If desired, drill a hole near the back corner of each shelf for routing power cords.

STEP 7: Drill holes for the all-thread hangers following the ceiling joist layout. Finish the shelves as desired. Nail the shelves to the cleats with 4d nails and then route the all-thread rod through the hooks. Tighten a nut onto the rod below each shelf to support it.

STEP 8: Use a level and carpenter's pencil to mark lines representing the top edges of the desktop cleats: 1½" below the desk surface. Note: Standard desktop height is 29 to 30" from the floor, while typing surfaces are typically 26 to 27". Cut and install the 1 × 2 cleats flush with the lines using a 3½" wood screw driven into each wall stud.

STEP 9: Cut two identical pieces of desktop stock to fit the closet dimensions, with a little bit of wiggle room for getting the stock in place (be sure to account for the ¾" thickness of the 1 × 2 nosing). Glue the pieces together on their bare faces using wood glue and a few 1¼" screws to clamp them together while the glue dries. Make sure the pieces are perfectly flush at their front edges.

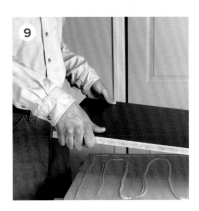

STEP 10: Install the desktop. If desired, drill a large hole (1½"-dia. or so) through the desktop for routing cords, using a hole saw or spade bit. Cut, sand, and finish 1 × 2 stock for the decorative nosing. Install the nosing with wood glue and 2" finish nails, keeping it flush with the desk surface. Set the desktop onto the cleats; its weight will keep it securely in place.

Custom Laundry Center

Laundry rooms commonly lack space to spread out and keep your cleaning products organized and effective lighting that makes working in the space easy. This is because most laundry rooms are afterthoughts in home design, utility spaces that are not so much designed as carved out or tacked on. But fortunately, with the steps that follow, you don't need to deal with the annoyance of a ill-suited laundry area any longer.

This self-contained laundry center is ideal for handling even a big busy home's worth of dirty clothes. It functions like a room within a room, adding both storage space and task lighting for what can otherwise be a disagreeable task. It is built from a base cabinet and butcher block countertop on one side of a 24"-wide, 7'-tall stub wall, and a bank of wall cabinets on the other side of the wall. The cabinets are specifically designed to fit above a standard washer and dryer (if you have stackables, you'll need to adjust the layout).

It may not be the ritziest material, but the tileboard specified for cladding the surfaces in the project is durable and easy to clean—essential features in an area where some dirt and bumps are just par for the course. The maple trim keeps things looking as nice as any other room in the house.

Word to the wise: If this center is going into a room that didn't house the laundry before arrange for and have installed the hookups for both appliances before you build. If you are not experienced with plumbing and wiring, hire a plumber and electrician to run any new drain, supply, dryer vent, or electrical service lines.

WHAT YOU NEED:

MATERIALS

- (1) 4 × 8' × ½" plywood or OSB (wall sheathing)
- (1) 4 × 8' × ¾" plywood or OSB (ceiling)
- (3) 4 × 8' sheets tileboard
- (3) Recessed canister light with trim kit (optional)
- (1) 24" clothes rod with mounting hardware

- 1 × 2", 1 × 4", and 1 × 6" maple
- (2) 30" 2-door uppers
- Electrical box (optional)
- Switch (optional)
- ¹⁴⁄₂ romex (optional)
- Switch plate (optional)
- Panel adhesive
- Drywall or deck screws

- Nails
- (4) 1½ × 3½ × 96" pine
- (1) 34½ × 36" base cabinet
- (2) 12 × 30 × 30" wall cabinets
- (1) 1½ × 25 × 36" butcherblock countertop

TOOLS

- Tape measure
- Level
- Pencil
- Square

- Drill/driver and bits
- Powder-actuated nailer
- Hammer or pneumatic nailer
- Jigsaw

- Circular saw
- Miter saw
- Eye and ear protection
- Work gloves

CUSTOM LAUNDRY CENTER CUT LIST

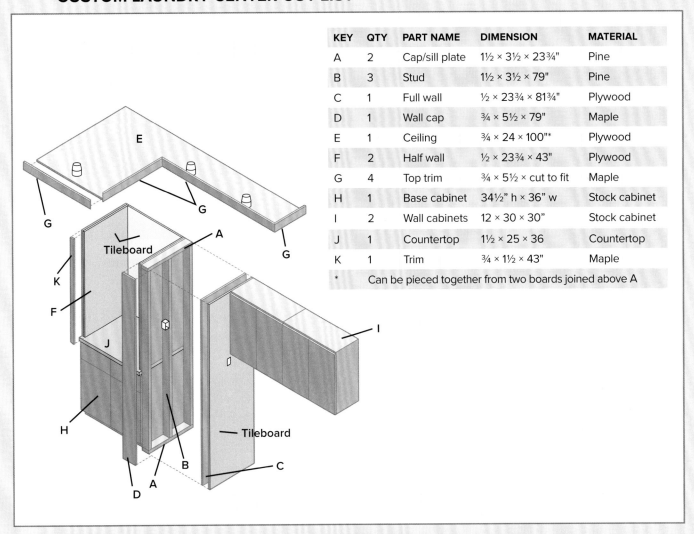

KEY	QTY	PART NAME	DIMENSION	MATERIAL
A	2	Cap/sill plate	1½ × 3½ × 23¾"	Pine
B	3	Stud	1½ × 3½ × 79"	Pine
C	1	Full wall	½ × 23¾ × 81¾"	Plywood
D	1	Wall cap	¾ × 5½ × 79"	Maple
E	1	Ceiling	¾ × 24 × 100"*	Plywood
F	2	Half wall	½ × 23¾ × 43"	Plywood
G	4	Top trim	¾ × 5½ × cut to fit	Maple
H	1	Base cabinet	34½" h × 36" w	Stock cabinet
I	2	Wall cabinets	12 × 30 × 30"	Stock cabinet
J	1	Countertop	1½ × 25 × 36	Countertop
K	1	Trim	¾ × 1½ × 43"	Maple

* Can be pieced together from two boards joined above A

How to Build a Custom Laundry Center

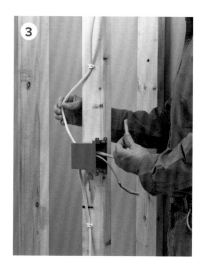

STEP 1: Attach the 23¾" base sill plate for the 7' × 24" stub wall perpendicular to an existing wall, allowing space between the stub wall and the corner for your base cabinet (36" in this case). Use pressure-treated wood if you're installing the laundry center in a basement. Fasten the plate with a powder-actuated nailer and concrete nails.

STEP 2: After toenailing the studs to the base plate (and facenailing the stud next to the wall if possible) nail the 23¾" cap plate to the top of the studs with 16d common nails, making sure the studs are plumb.

STEP 3: If you are installing overhead lighting, run cable from the power source through the studs and to an electrical switch box mounted to the wall frame. Install boxes for the light fixtures (don't hook up the wires yet). Hire an electrician to do this if you are not experienced with home wiring. (Note that you will need to apply for a permit and have your wiring inspected.) Also run sheathed cable from the electrical box and out through a hole in the wall cap plate. Run enough cable to reach the light fixtures. Here, the fixtures are wired in series: the power lead goes to the canister light over the counter, then runs to the other lights. If you prefer to switch the light independently, install a double gang box and cable for two switched circuits.

STEP 4: Install the base cabinet between the stub wall and the corner, making sure it is level and securely attached to at least one wall.

STEP 5: Install the butcher block countertop by drilling extra-large guide holes through the nailing strips on the base cabinet. Attach the countertop with a short screws and washers. This allows the material to move as it expands and contracts.

STEP 6: Cut plywood to match the width of the stub wall and the height from the countertop to the top of the wall opposite the stub wall.

STEP 7: Clad the stub wall on both sides with plywood, making a cutout for the switch box. The plywood on the countertop side should rest on the countertop. Shim underneath the plywood on the other side of the stub wall to avoid direct contact with the floor and possible water damage.

STEP 8: Measure the wall surfaces and cut tileboard to match the dimensions. Coat the back of the tileboard with panel adhesive. Position the tileboard on the plywood wall surfaces and rub aggressively with balled-up towels to help seat the tileboard into the adhesive.

STEP 9: Attach a ledger to the wall leaving space for the upper cabinets to be mounted with their tops flush to the top of the stub wall. The side of the cabinets should butt the stub wall. Screw the cabinets through their mounting strips, into wall studs. If the exposed cabinet end is not finished, install an end panel to match the cabinet type or fabricate one from ¼" plywood.

STEP 10: Cut the plywood for the ceiling to the size and shape of the space (if the ceiling is more than 96", make it in two pieces, so the seam falls in the middle of the stub wall top plate). Cut tileboard and attach it to the plywood face. The ceiling here is 24" wide above the cabinet, cut back to 18" wide over the wall cabinets. This creates a 6" overhang above the cabinets so that an undercabinet light fixture can be mounted.

STEP 11: Plan the locations for the light fixtures and mount the housings and ceiling boxes to the side opposite the tileboard.

STEP 12: Position the ceiling assembly over the laundry center and screw it to the stub wall top plate and the cabinet sides.

STEP 13: Turn the main power off and make the wiring connections at the light fixtures and at the switch. If you're not comfortable handling this electrical work, hire a licensed electrician. You will need a wiring inspection before making the final hookup at the power source.

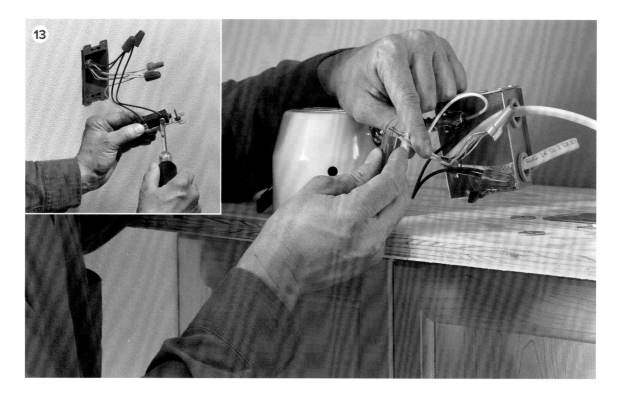

STEP 14: Measure and cut top trim pieces of 1 × 4" maple. Miter the ends and install the trim with wood glue and finish nails. A pneumatic nailer will make the process go easier and faster.

STEP 15: Measure and rip vertical trim pieces for the stub wall edge and the opposite wall. For a more finished look, round over the edges of the vertical trim pieces slightly. Install as you did with the top trim. Level and hook up the washer and dryer.

Compact Laundry Center

Although there may be no scientific evidence to prove it, we all know that there's a direct correlation between the quality of a laundry room space and how much we dread doing the laundry. Cramped, cluttered, or poorly arranged utility spaces slow the work and add a general sense of unpleasantness. And things get complicated when you can't complete the laundry tasks in the laundry room—you have to hang up your sweaters to dry over the bathtub and do all the folding on the kitchen table.

If this sounds familiar, you'll be glad to know that it doesn't take much to turn an ordinary laundry area into an efficient storage and work center. Nor does it take a lot of space. The project shown here requires only about nine feet of wall area, including where the washer and dryer go. And with a few extra feet available on a nearby wall, you can add a hideaway ironing board that folds up into a recessed cabinet when not in use.

The center makes best use of prefab cabinetry and easy-to-clean (and inexpensive) melamine surfaces. The look of the finished installation is simple, crisp, and understated. That means the center will complement just about any home décor and look nice for a long time to come.

WHAT YOU NEED:

How to Build a Compact Laundry Center

STEP 1: Mark the cabinet locations on the wall, including level lines to represent the cabinets' top edges. Standard cabinet height is 84" above the floor, but make sure the washer door won't block the hanging shelf. Use a stud finder to locate and mark all of the wall studs behind the cabinet locations.

STEP 2: Assemble the cabinets, if necessary. Position each cabinet with its top edge flush to the level line, drill pilot holes, and fasten through the back panel and into the wall studs with at least four 3½" heavy-duty wood screws (or install according to the manufacturer's directions).

STEP 3: Cut pieces of ¾" melamine-covered particleboard for the hanging shelf. Cut the top and bottom pieces equal to the cabinet depth by the cabinet width, minus 1½". Cut the side pieces equal to the cabinet depth by the overall shelf height (as desired). Cut the back panel equal to the cabinet depth by the shelf height, minus 1½" in both directions.

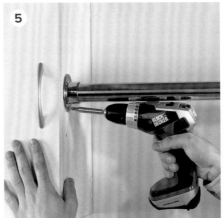

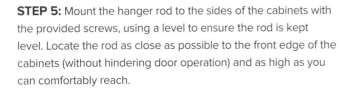

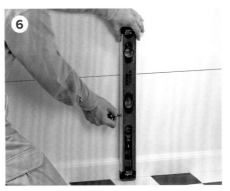

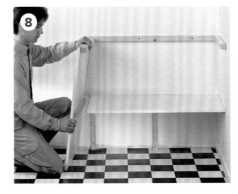

STEP 4: Construct the hanging shelf with polyurethane glue and 2" drywall screws. Cover the exposed edges and screw heads with melamine-laminate edge tape. When the glue has cured, mount the shelf to the bottom cabinet panel with 1¼" drywall screws driven through pilot holes.

STEP 5: Mount the hanger rod to the sides of the cabinets with the provided screws, using a level to ensure the rod is kept level. Locate the rod as close as possible to the front edge of the cabinets (without hindering door operation) and as high as you can comfortably reach.

STEP 6: Mark the layout of the countertop and shelf unit onto the wall. Draw level lines at 34½" and at the desired height for the shelf top minus ¾". Draw plumb lines for the end panel at 46½ and 47¼" from the side wall and for the shelf support at 22⅞ and 23⅝" from the side wall. Mark wall stud locations.

STEP 7: Following the layout lines, cut and install 2 × 2 wall cleats for the countertop along the back and side walls. Fasten the cleats to the wall studs with 3½" deck screws. Cut and install 1 × 2 cleats for the shelf, shelf support, and end panel using 2½" deck screws or drywall screws.

STEP 8: Build the end panel and shelf to size at 34½" long by the countertop depth minus ¾". Cut the shelf at 46½" long by the same width as the end panel. Add a 2 × 2 cleat flush with the top edge of the end panel. Fasten the shelf and end panel to the wall cleats with polyurethane glue and 2¼" finish nails. Fasten through the end panel and into the shelf edge with 2" screws.

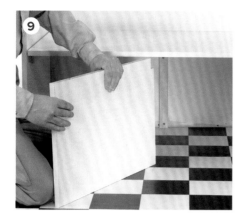

STEP 9: Cut the shelf support to fit underneath the shelf. Notch the back edge to fit around the 1 × 2 wall cleat, then fasten the support to the cleat and shelf with glue and 2¼" finish nails.

STEP 10: Prepare the countertop by cutting a stiffener panel from ¾" particleboard to fit inside the edges on the underside of the countertop. Fasten the panel with wood glue and 1¼" screws. If desired, install an end cap kit onto the end opposite the side wall following the manufacturer's directions. Set the countertop in place and secure it to the 2 × 2 cleats with 2" screws.

STEP 11: Begin the ironing board cabinet installation by locating two adjacent wall studs and drawing level lines to mark the top and bottom of the wall opening. Make sure there's no wiring or plumbing inside the wall cavity, then cut the drywall along the stud edges and the level lines using a drywall saw.

STEP 12: Fit the cabinet into the wall opening and secure it to the wall studs using the recommended screws. NOTE: Add a drop hook on the inside of the cabinet door for hanging up ironed clothes (inset). The hook drops down against the door when not in use.

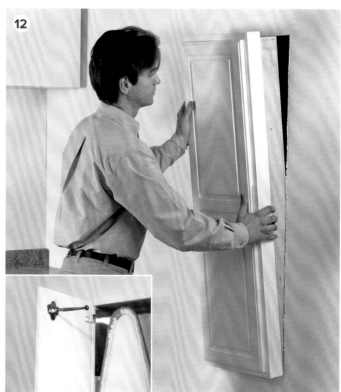

Hobby Center

All too often, homeowners try to cram space for their favorite crafting or art activities into other areas, like a corner of the garage or a guest bedroom closet, where a fun pursuit becomes so much less fun to do. It's a dilemma, but one that is easily solved.

The answer is to dedicate an area to the hobby you love, and the most space-efficient way to do that is to take over the corner of a larger room. This hobby center can be tucked into the far side of a living room, a sunny corner in your master bedroom, or even a little-used portion of a large kitchen. Everything about the design and how it is laid out is focused on perfect efficiency and providing comfort in the least amount of space possible.

Although it includes a sophisticated elements—an abundance of storage space courtesy of prefab cabinets and a simple yet accommodating desktop—you won't have to go to contractor's school to handle constructing this center. Just measure twice and cut once, and the rest is pretty much straightforward installation. The laminate desktop configuration gives you both room to spread out a project or stage supplies left and right, and three access points (center, left, and right) for you to move a large project around or have helpers.

WHAT YOU NEED:

MATERIALS

- (2) 24 × 34½" base cabinets
- (2) 18 × 30" upper cabinets
- L-shape 12 × 25 × 72" countertop
- (1) 24 × 30" corner cabinet
- (2) 2 × 3" × 8 pine
- Drywall or deck screws
- Finish nails

TOOLS

- Pencil
- Tape measure
- Level or laser level
- Drill/driver
- Miter saw

HOBBY CENTER CUT LIST

KEY	QTY	PART NAME	DIMENSION	MATERIAL
A	2	Wall cleat	1½ × 2½ × 40"	Pine
B	1	Diagonal cleat	1½ × 2½ × 59"	Pine
C	1	L-shape countertop	1½ × 25 × 72"	Walnut

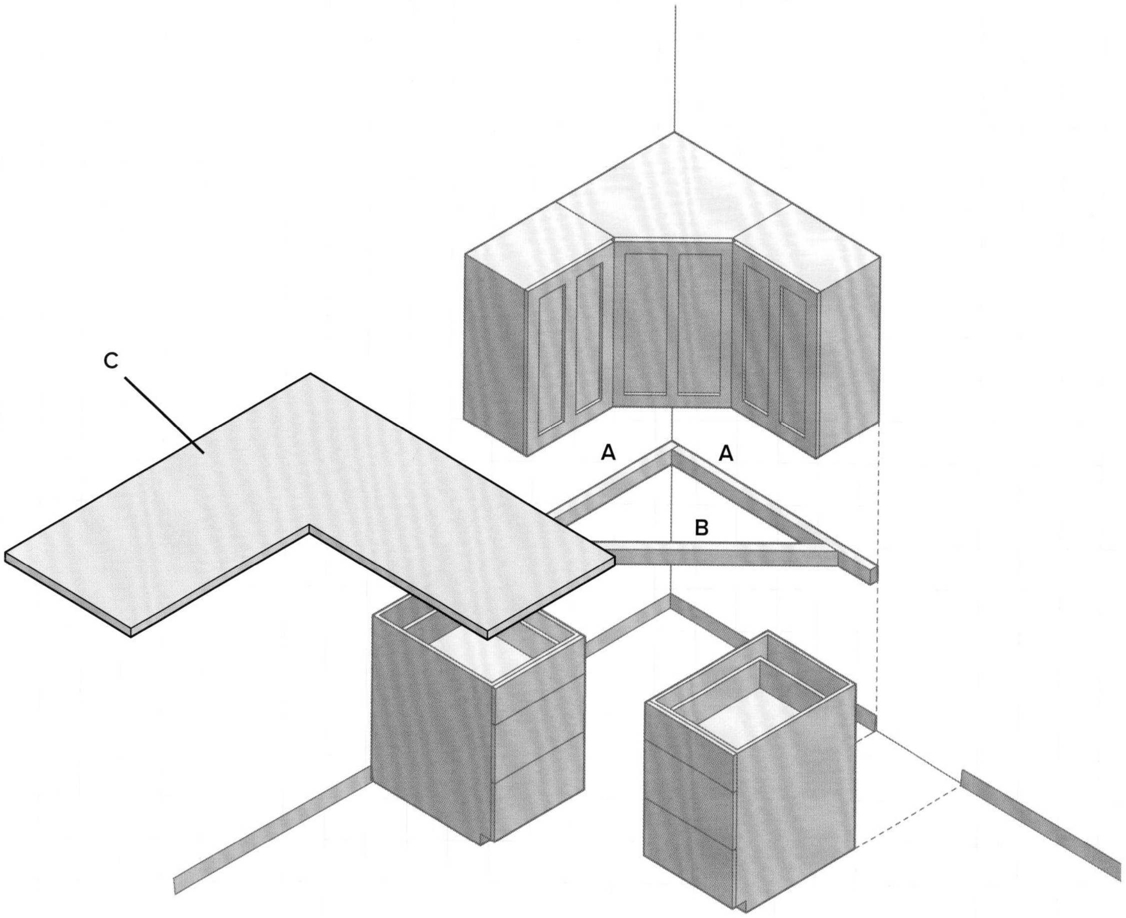

How to Build a Hobby Center

STEP 1: Measure and mark a level line for the upper cabinets 52½" above the floor, and projecting 42" out on each side from the wall corner.

STEP 2: Locate and mark the wall studs below the level line. Screw a temporary ledger to the wall studs right below the level line, to support the cabinets during installation.

STEP 3: Measure along the top of the base molding from the corner, marking at 42" and 60" on the base trim. (This is the location of each base cabinet.) Use a combination square, and mark plumb lines down to the floor. The 18" of base/shoe molding between the lines will be removed to accept the base cabinets. In the corner, measure up 34½" (the height of the base cabinet) from the floor and mark each side of the wall.

STEP 4: Transfer the location of the wall studs to the insides of the cabinets for future reference, while you're holding the cabinets up in place. Subtract the width of the cabinet sides when calculating.

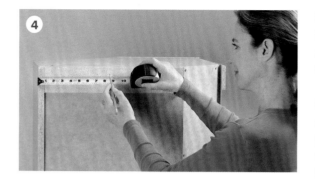

STEP 5: Set the upper center cabinet on the ledger in the corner of the wall and screw it to studs, but do not drive the screws all the way (this allows for a little fine tuning).

STEP 6: Repeat for each end cabinet. Before fully sinking the wall screws, clamp the cabinets together, drill pilot holes in the cabinet sides or face frames, and screw them together. Be sure the fronts of all the cabinets are flush. Complete the process by driving all wall screws tightly against the cabinet back. Install the cabinet doors.

STEP 7: Position the base cabinets at the layout lines and screw them to the wall studs.

STEP 8: The desktop will need to be supported by a 3-piece ledger construction. Cut and install 2 × 3 ledgers along the wall, fastening with two 3" screws into the wall studs. Note that the second piece overlaps the first piece and must be cut 1½" shorter to fit. Measure and cut the first piece to fit between the wall and the inside edge of a base cabinet. A piece just shy of 42" should fit.

STEP 9: Cut a 2 × 3 diagonal ledger brace to 59" with opposing miters.

STEP 10: Predrill and preset screws in the mitered ends of the diagonal brace then install.

STEP 11: Have a custom desktop made to fit over the cabinets and into the corner, or make your own. With the aid of a helper, place the desktop on top of the base cabinet/ledger system. Fine-tune the desktop placement onto the layout marks.

STEP 12: Fasten the desktop from inside the base cabinets as well as through the ledger system's diagonal brace. Fastening through the diagonal brace requires predrilling and installing screws on an angle. Be careful not to puncture the top surface of the desktop.

STEP 13: Caulk between the cabinet edges and the wall as necessary. Clad the base cabinet bottoms with base molding as necessary and prime and paint the ledger boards the same as the wall color. Install an undercabinet light beneath the upper cabinets to provide focused task lighting.

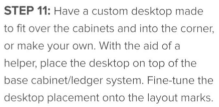

Media Bar

No man cave (or woman cave, for that matter) is complete without an entertainment center, and without some semblance of a bar full of refreshments and snacks. This project combines the best of both worlds in a compact, handsome package just right for those homeowners who might not have a large bonus room, basement, or garage to dedicate to such an entertainment space.

The structure is confined to one wall, where you can hang a flat-screen TV, park a bachelor refrigerator, and store plenty of edibles, glasses, and entertainment extras in the abundant cabinet space. The false wall on which the TV is placed leaves space behind it to run cables and keep them hidden. Because even a man cave should feature some style.

But perhaps the best benefit is that the final appearance looks like a custom unit built by a master carpenter. That's the benefit of opting for readymade cabinetry. Not only do these stock units make everything quicker and easier, they also cut down on the skills and time the project will require, leaving you more hours to just enjoy your favorite show—and a craft brew or two!

WHAT YOU NEED:

MATERIALS

- (5) 2 × 4" × 8' pine
- (2) 1 × 4" × 8' pine
- 1¼", 2", and 2½" wood screws
- Panel adhesive
- (1) ½" × 4 × 8' finish-grade plywood
- (3) 24" base cabinets
- (2) 24" wall cabinets
- (1) 25½" × 8' countertop
- Metal bracket

TOOLS

- Studfinder
- Carpenter's pencil
- Table saw or circular saw and straightedge
- Jigsaw
- Power drill and bits
- Level
- 2" hole saw
- Caulk gun
- Eye and ear protection
- Work gloves

MEDIA BAR CUT LIST

KEY	QTY	PART NAME	DIMENSION	MATERIAL
A	5	Wall frame studs	1½ × 3½ × 60"	Pine
B	3	Wall frame cleats	¾ × 3½ × 47"	Pine
C	1	Base cabinet cover panel	½ × 24 × 30"	Birch plywood
D	1	Left frame side cover panel	½ × 4¼ × 60"	Birch plywood
E	1	Right frame side cover panel	½ × 4¼ × 20"	Birch plywood
F	1	Back splash panels	½ × 20 × 48"	Birch plywood
G	1	Wall frame front cover panels	½ × 48 × 60"	Birch plywood
H	1	Wall cabinet side cover panel	½ × 8⅝ × 40"	Birch plywood
I	1	Front toe kick	½ × 4½" × 24"	Pine
J	1 or 2	Side toe kick	½ × 4½" × 24"	Pine

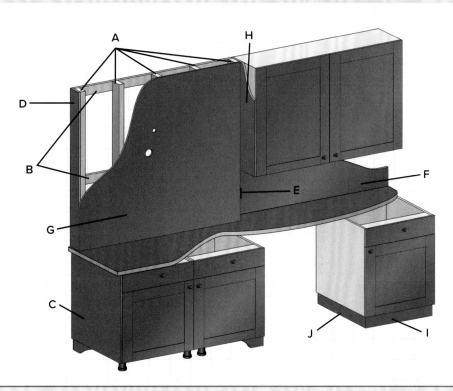

How to Build a Media Bar

STEP 1: Locate and mark the wall stud locations. Follow the manufacturers' instructions to assemble the wall and base cabinet frames if not preassembled. If the doors and drawers are not attached to the cabinets, wait to install them until after the cover panels are attached.

STEP 2: Fasten the two wall cabinets using the method recommended by the manufacturer for the cabinet. Here, a metal bracket is attached to the wall and then the cabinet is fastened to the metal bracket.

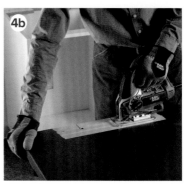

STEP 3: Line up the base cabinets a few feet away from the wall, positioning them in the order that they will be installed. Measure the distance to the wall outlet from the end of the cabinets and from the floor and transfer those measurements to the back of the cabinet to mark the outlet location.

STEP 4: Trace outlines for the access holes in the back panel and top spreader on the cabinet that will be installed in front of the wall outlet. Drill ⅜" saw-blade starter holes at each corner of the outline. Use a jigsaw to cut a 3"-wide × 5"-tall hole through the cabinet back panel exactly where the outlet will be located.

STEP 5: Cut the countertop access hole. Attach masking tape to the countertop to help prevent chipping the surface when it is cut. Mark the access notch outline on the countertop. Drill ⅜"-dia. saw blade starter hole and cut the notch with a jigsaw.

STEP 6: Attach the countertop to the cabinets. Drive 1 ⅝" screws through the cabinet top and into the countertop. Be careful not to overdrive the screws and break through the top surface of the countertop.

STEP 7: Cut the 2 × 4 wall frame posts and 1 × 4 cleats to length and assemble them with 2" wood screws. Place this wall frame on the countertop and against the wall cabinet. Screw the wall frame to the drywall with 2½" drywall screws driven through the wall frame cleats and into studs. Drive three screws into each stud.

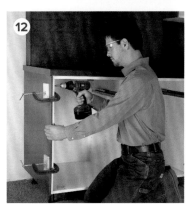

STEP 8: Route speaker cables or other component cables from other areas of the room behind the wall frame. Cover the frame with the finish panels. (Cables that run between the TV, sound bar speaker, and components in the cabinet are routed after the cabinet construction is complete.) Each panel is attached with screws and panel adhesive; the screws are driven through the inside face of the cabinet or wall frame.

STEP 9: Measure the width of the space below the wall cabinets and divide that measurement by two. This is backsplash panel width. Cut the backsplash panels to size by cutting from the back, with masking tape over the cut line. Use an 80-tooth-per-inch plywood blade. Cut openings in the panel to fit around any wall outlet. Attach the backsplash panels with panel adhesive.

STEP 10: Cut the two frame-side cover panels to size, using a circular saw and straightedge guide. Apply panel adhesive to the back face of each panel, clamp them to the wall frame, and secure them with panel adhesive and 1⅝" screws. Drill a ⅛" countersunk pilot hole.

STEP 11: Measure the distance from the face of the front panel to the front edge of the wall cabinet. Add the thickness of the door to determine the width of the wall cabinet side cover panel.

STEP 12: Attach the wall- and base-cabinet side panels. Clamp the panel to the cabinet side and drive 1" screws through the inside face of the cabinet side. Install the toe kicks, doors, and drawers.

STEP 13: Use a 2" hole saw to bore an access hole through the wall frame front panel. This hole should be located directly above the notch in the countertop and close to the TV mounting bracket so that the TV will conceal it. Drive the mounting bracket anchor screws into the wall frame posts. If you are installing a speaker above the TV, drill a ¾" hole behind the speaker location to route the speaker cable.

STEP 14: Fish the component cables and speaker cable through the access holes and behind the front panels. Follow the manufacturer instructions to secure the TV to the mounting bracket and mount the speaker.

Towel Tower

Keeping towels in order is key to keeping bathroom clutter to a minimum. That can be a monumental challenge in a busy household full of people, because these are daily use textiles. With a spouse and children on hectic schedules, you may have four or more towels in constant rotation. Add that to the usual bathroom debris—clothing odds and ends, extra toilet paper, and more— and you have a real need for some organizational help in a common bathroom. Enter this towel tower.

With the help of an over-the-refrigerator cabinet (what is also know as a "bridge cabinet") and a few other widely available bits and pieces, you can build the perfect organizer and one that looks unique and attractive. Suitable even for small bathrooms, this towel tower adds texture and color to the space. If that wasn't enough, the board that tops the bottom cabinet adds seating.

The beadboard backing for this project is made with painted ⅜" tongue-and-groove pine, sometimes called "carsiding." The look is a little bit country, but you can use whatever color of paint or wood finish you desire to tailor the look to your own design tastes. Also keep in mind that despite its name, this tower will work just as well in large open hallway or common space that sees a lot of clothing clutter, or even a mudroom entryway, where it could corral outerwear and give visitors a place to take boots and shoes on and off.

WHAT YOU NEED:

MATERIALS

- ▸ 32 sq. ft. tongue-and-groove paneling
- ▸ (1) 15"h × 30"w × 24"d over-fridge cabinet
- ▸ (2) 1 × 6" × 8' pine
- ▸ 3' crown molding
- ▸ Half sheet ¾" MDF
- ▸ 12' quarter-round molding
- ▸ Towel hooks
- ▸ Fasteners
- ▸ Paint, stain, or other finish

TOOLS

- ▸ Tape measure
- ▸ Carpenter's pencil
- ▸ Router and bits
- ▸ Power drill and bits
- ▸ Circular saw
- ▸ Straightedge
- ▸ Level
- ▸ Hammer
- ▸ Paintbrush
- ▸ Pneumatic nailer (optional)
- ▸ Eye and ear protection
- ▸ Work gloves

CUSTOM LAUNDRY CENTER CUT LIST

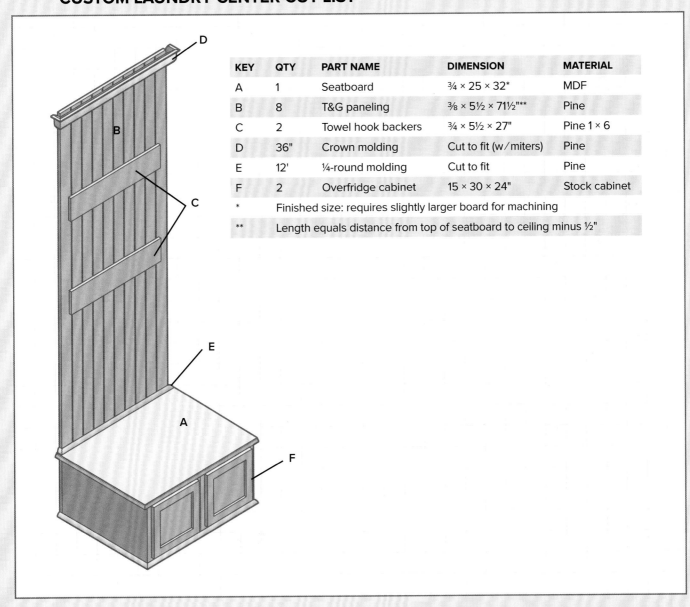

KEY	QTY	PART NAME	DIMENSION	MATERIAL
A	1	Seatboard	¾ × 25 × 32*	MDF
B	8	T&G paneling	⅜ × 5½ × 71½"**	Pine
C	2	Towel hook backers	¾ × 5½ × 27"	Pine 1 × 6
D	36"	Crown molding	Cut to fit (w/miters)	Pine
E	12'	¼-round molding	Cut to fit	Pine
F	2	Overfridge cabinet	15 × 30 × 24"	Stock cabinet
*		Finished size: requires slightly larger board for machining		
**		Length equals distance from top of seatboard to ceiling minus ½"		

How to Build a Towel Tower

STEP 1: Cut a piece of medium density fiberboard (MDF) 1" wider than the cabinet and a couple of inches longer front-to-back (here, 26" for the 24" cabinet). Use a piloted ogee or roundover bit in the router to shape the front and sides of the seat board.

STEP 2: Screw through the mounting strips on the cabinet top and into the underside of the seat board. The seat's back edge should be flush with the back edge of the cabinet and the overhang should be equal on both sides. Clamp the blank in location on the cabinet, then lay the cabinet on its back for better access.

STEP 3: Remove the baseboard and any other obstructions and shim underneath and behind the cabinet as needed to make it level and plumb. Screw the cabinet to the wall with 2" drywall screws, driven into studs.

STEP 4: Lay the beadboard out with tongues fit in grooves. Measure in one direction, half the width of base cabinet, from the midpoint line in the center board. Rip the outside boards as necessary to fit the project area.

STEP 5: Clamp a straightedge over a tongue-and-groove board, placing a piece of scrap plywood underneath as a backer. Rip cut the board to the correct thickness for the filler piece.

STEP 6: Use a level to extend plumb lines directly up the wall from the outside edges of the seat. Mark the stud locations on the seat and ceiling with tape. Begin installing the beadboard on the left side, with the left trimmed board. In most cases, the tongue will be preserved on this board and should be oriented inward.

STEP 7: Continue installing boards until you reach the right edge. Use plenty of adhesive and drive several nails when you hit a wall stud. If the beadboard joints don't fall on a stud, tack the board over a stud by face-nailing once at the top and once at the bottom. NOTE: The towel hook mounting boards will help hold the beadboard once attached at studs. Cut the towel hook boards to length from 1 × 6 stock and screw them in place.

STEP 8: Install quarter-round or base shoe molding at the top edge of the seat where it meets the beadboard. Tie the molding back to the wall with mitered returns. Attach crown molding at the top, creating mitered returns at the ends.

STEP 9: Finish the structure as desired. Measure and mark for the placement of the towel hooks. Screw them to the backers.

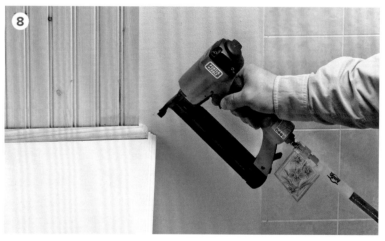

Crown Molding Shelf

Want to build an elegant, eye-catching shelf that is just the right dimension to store and display your collectibles in sight but out of the way? If so, this shelf is for you. It is a built-up, wall-mounted platform that is a fun combination of rough and finish carpentry, totally doable regardless of how much experience you have working with wood.

This crown-molding shelf is essentially a built-up box beam with crown molding as the featured trim. It is a sophisticated three-part shelf similar in assembly to cornice molding made with pine and pine moldings. It is wonderfully customizable; not only can you choose from an amazing diversity of crown molding styles, you can also paint the shelves any color of the rainbow or stain or finish them to leverage the character of the wood.

Hang new shelves at just about any height, although they naturally look more comfortable higher up on the wall. The most pleasing location will be slightly above eye level for the average person in the house. Locating the shelves so the bottom edge rests on top of a door casing is a good strategy and a unique look. Not only are these built-in shelves totally homemade, the usage is adaptable to different needs and tastes. For example, you can wrap the entire room with multiples of these shelves, or place the shelf on one wall.

WHAT YOU NEED:

MATERIALS

- 3½" GRK screws
- 150-grit sandpaper
- 2¾" flathead wood screws
- 6d finish nails

- Panel adhesive
- Wood putty
- Paint, stain, or other finish
- Crown molding

- Pine or oak boards
- 2 x 4s
- Eye and ear protection
- Work gloves

TOOLS

- Table saw
- Miter saw
- Palm sander
- Level or laser level

- Power drill and bits
- Tape measure
- Square
- Caulk gun

- Nail set
- Putty knife
- Paintbrush

CROWN MOLDING SHELF CUT LIST

KEY	QTY	PART NAME	DIMENSION	MATERIAL
A	1	Shelf top	¾ × 7¼" × length	Pine or oak
B	1	Shelf bottom	¾ × 2¾" × length	Pine or oak
C	1	Shelf front	¾ × 4½" × length	Pine or oak
D	1*	Crown	¾ × 4¼" × length	Crown molding
E	1	Ledger	1½ × 3½" × length	Pine
F	1 or 2	Filler (opt.)	¾ × 2¾ × 3½"	Pine or oak

*   Make mitered return if end of shelf is open

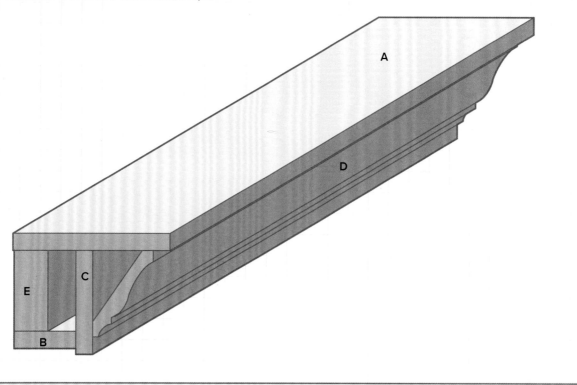

How to Construct a Crown Molding Shelf

STEP 1: Use a laser level to create a level reference line for the shelf ledger installation. Mark the location of the bottom edge of the ledger, making sure to allow room for the bottom panel above the door trim and for the full height of the finished project. NOTE: If you want your shelving flush with the top of a door or window casing and you find it is close to level (within ¼"), use the highest opening as the control point for your layout and fill the gap that'll be created over the other windows with caulk.

STEP 2: Cut a straight 2 × 4 to length and use a stud finder to locate wall studs in the installation area. Mark them just below the level line.

STEP 3: Apply panel adhesive to the back of the ledger and position it so the bottom edge falls just above the level line and the ends are in the correct spot. Drive a pair of 3½" GRK screws through the ledger and into the studs at each location.

STEP 4: Install molding pieces from the bottom and work your way up. Rip wood for the bottom panel to width (2¾" here) and cut it to length. Finish sand all wood parts with 150-grit sandpaper before installing.

STEP 5: On the bottom strip, drill a countersunk pilot hole every 12", located in a line ¾" in from the back edge of the strip. Attach the bottom strip to the ledger with panel adhesive and 2¾" flathead wood screws.

STEP 6: Crosscut the top panel to length and then attach it to the top of the ledger with panel adhesive and 6d finish nails. The ends should be flush with the bottom strip ends, and the top panel should be butted cleanly against the wall.

STEP 7: Measure the distance from the front face of the ledger to the front edge of the bottom strip and cut a few spacers to this length from scrap. Attach the spacers to the face of the ledger at several spots along the length of the ledger. These will ensure that the front panel is vertical when it is positioned against the spacers.

STEP 8: Rip and crosscut the front panel to width and length. Press it against the spacers so the top edge is flush against the underside of the top panel and all ends are aligned. Drill pilot holes and drive 6d finish nails through the front panel and into the edge of the bottom strip. (You can also nail at the spacer locations if you wish.)

STEP 9: Drill pilot holes and drive nails through the top panel and into the top edge of the front panel. Set the nail heads with a nail set. Putty over them, sand, and paint or finish the shelves as desired.

STEP 10: Cut crown molding to length and fit it between the top panel and the front panel. Attach with 6d finish nails, paint or stain, as desired.

Metric Conversion Chart

CONVERTING MEASUREMENTS

TO CONVERT:	TO:	MULTIPLY BY:
Inches	Millimeters	25.4
Inches	Centimeters	2.54
Feet	Meters	0.305
Yards	Meters	0.914
Square inches	Square centimeters	6.45
Square feet	Square meters	0.093
Square yards	Square meters	0.836
Cubic inches	Cubic centimeters	16.4
Cubic feet	Cubic meters	0.0283
Cubic yards	Cubic meters	0.765
Pounds	Kilograms	0.454

TO CONVERT:	TO:	MULTIPLY BY:
Millimeters	Inches	0.039
Centimeters	Inches	0.394
Meters	Feet	3.28
Meters	Yards	1.09
Square centimeters	Square inches	0.155
Square meters	Square feet	10.8
Square meters	Square yards	1.2
Cubic centimeters	Cubic inches	0.061
Cubic meters	Cubic feet	35.3
Cubic meters	Cubic yards	1.31
Kilograms	Pounds	2.2

LUMBER DIMENSIONS

NOMINAL–US	ACTUAL–US (IN INCHES)	METRIC
1 × 2	¾ × 1½	19 × 38 mm
1 × 3	¾ × 2½	19 × 64 mm
1 × 4	¾ × 3½	19 × 89 mm
1 × 6	¾ × 5½	19 × 140 mm
1 × 8	¾ × 7¼	19 × 184 mm
1 × 10	¾ × 9¼	19 × 235 mm
1 × 12	¾ × 11¼	19 × 286 mm
2 × 2	1½ × 1½	38 × 38 mm
2 × 3	1½ × 2½	38 × 64 mm

NOMINAL–US	ACTUAL–US (IN INCHES)	METRIC
2 × 4	1½ × 3½	38 × 89 mm
2 × 6	1½ × 5½	38 × 140 mm
2 × 8	1½ × 7¼	38 × 184 mm
2 × 10	1½ × 9¼	38 × 235 mm
2 × 12	1½ × 11¼	38 × 286 mm
4 × 4	3½ × 3½	89 × 89 mm
4 × 6	3½ × 5½	89 × 140 mm
6 × 6	5½ × 5½	140 × 140 mm
8 × 8	7¼ × 7¼	184 × 184 mm

METRIC PLYWOOD

STANDARD SHEATHING GRADE	SANDED GRADE
7.5 mm (⁵⁄₁₆")	6 mm (⁴⁄₁₇")
9.5 mm (³⁄₈")	8 mm (⁵⁄₁₆")
12.5 mm (½")	11 mm (⁷⁄₁₆")
15.5 mm (⅝")	14 mm (⁹⁄₁₆")
18.5 mm (¾")	17 mm (⅔")
20.5 mm (¹³⁄₁₆")	19 mm (¾")
22.5 mm (⅞")	21 mm (¹³⁄₁₆")
25.5 mm (1")	24 mm (¹⁵⁄₁₆")

COUNTERBORE, SHANK, & PILOT HOLE DIAMETERS (INCHES)

SCREW SIZE	COUNTERBORE DIAMETER FOR SCREW HEAD	CLEARANCE HOLE FOR SCREW SHANK	PILOT HOLE DIAMETER	
			HARD WOOD	SOFT WOOD
#1	(⁹⁄₆₄)	⁵⁄₆₄	³⁄₆₄	¹⁄₃₂
#2	¼	³⁄₃₂	³⁄₆₄	¹⁄₃₂
#3	¼	⁷⁄₆₄	¹⁄₁₆	³⁄₆₄
#4	¼	⅛	¹⁄₁₆	³⁄₆₄
#5	¼	⅛	⁵⁄₆₄	¹⁄₁₆
#6	⁵⁄₁₆	⁹⁄₆₄	³⁄₃₂	⁵⁄₆₄
#7	⁵⁄₁₆	⁵⁄₃₂	³⁄₃₂	⁵⁄₆₄
#8	³⁄₈	¹¹⁄₆₄	⅛	³⁄₃₂
#9	³⁄₈	¹¹⁄₆₄	⅛	³⁄₃₂
#10	³⁄₈	³⁄₁₆	⅛	⁷⁄₆₄
#11	½	³⁄₁₆	⁵⁄₃₂	⁹⁄₆₄
#12	½	⁷⁄₃₂	⁹⁄₆₄	⅛

Index